DEEPER

WITH BLACKFORD

Andy Blackford

Illustrations by Rico

Book designed and
produced by the DIVER Group

Printed by Emirates Printing Press,
PO Box 5106, Al Quoz, Dubai, UAE.

ISBN: 0 946020 32 9

Foreword

What more apt description could there possibly be for this, the introduction to the long-awaited second volume of Blackford's diving memoires?

For, since the publication of Volume One in 1985, Blackford has indeed moved *foreword*. And the diving fraternity has moved *foreword* with him.

By abandoning his twin-hose set in early 1998, he blazed a trail for the rest of us – a trail towards a glittering future of innovative design and advanced technology.

When, two years later, he hung up his horse-collar ABLJ, the diving world followed unquestioningly.

Last year he agreed to test-fly the ironically-named 'drysuit' and voices were raised in traditional circles: "Stop! Enough is enough! Progress is one thing, but surely there must be limits?"

Yet he pressed on undaunted and already more than a hundred so-called drysuits are in everyday use.

The true pioneers of our sport can be counted on the fingers of one hand: Cousteau; Hass; Hass. Well, actually, less than one hand.

But if there is a thumb, then Andy Blackford is most definitely it.

PERSONAL TIMES

Blackford's world –
and welcome to it

"Two-thirds of the Earth's surface is covered by water. So it's Blackford 2, Tolstoy 1."

The Times Literary Supplement

Toe be or not toe be a diver?

I BLAME the Toe. It was the Toe that started it. Big toe, left foot. It was drunk, frankly. Hardly surprising – it had been drinking from six o'clock through to midnight in the Bovisand bar. I'd watched it happen, with that sinking, helpless sensation that always accompanies the Inevitable in action.

How well I knew my Toe. We'd been together a long time. I knew its strengths and its weaknesses – and among the latter was its inordinate fondness for strong drink. Once it started, there was simply no stopping it. You just stood and watched; and when even that was rendered impractical, you just watched.

How we got back to the dormitory that night I'll never know. The Toe wove this way and that, accelerating and slowing without warning, lurching and swaying in the most disorientating fashion and completely ignoring the helpful advice I tried to offer it.

In fact, we might have negotiated the hill to the dormitory without serious incident had not the Toe decided to attempt an elaborate dance step to the rhythm of *I Wish I Could Shimmy Like My Sister Kate*, just as it was mounting a particularly challenging kerb.

I actually heard it break.

I managed to steer it, half-conscious, into the dormitory and on to my bunk.

There, it crawled down to the very foot of the bed like a wounded cat, curled up and passed out.

Next morning, I was awakened by waves of excruciating pain from the end of my leg. I hobbled to the Medical Centre where a nice young man bound up the Toe in a tubular bandage, ingeniously applying it with a gynaecological speculum.

3

"For years I didn't twig what this thing was really for," he explained cheerfully. "Slept through the lecture, most likely. Still, it's perfect for toes, so who gives a monkey's?"

The treatment was free. I should have known there'd be a catch. "Look here," he dropped in casually, "you seem like a fit sort of bloke. Ever had a bend?" I hadn't.

"It's just that a friend of mine is doing a bit of research into decompression illness. He's always on the look-out for experienced divers to act as 'controls' in his experiments. Why don't you give him a bell when you get back to London? I'm sure he could use you.

I must have had that "What's in it for me?" look, because he continued: "You never know, you might even be helping to save the lives of your fellow divers." Still I must have looked sceptical, because he added: "Or your own life, for that matter. You never know."

A week later, I lay on his friend's couch, unrecognisable beneath a writhing mass of electrodes, as he pumped saline solution into my thigh and stared at a bank of video monitors.

"Oh, great," he muttered. "Great! That's bloody typical, is that. Frankly, I don't know why I bother." When he tore off the electrodes, it was like having Giant Haystacks tidy up your bikini line with live leeches.

"Anything the matter?" I managed, through clenched jaws.

"Noooo, nothing's the matter," he sneered. (At some time in his career, he'd acted as locum for the Abominable Doctor Phibes.) "It's just that you're a bloody useless control. You've got a bloody PFO. I've just wasted an hour of my time. Why didn't you bloody tell me?"

"Tell you…?"

"That you've got a hole in the heart!"

I'll never forget the feeling this news produced in me. I felt hot and cold at the same time, like drowning in boiling ice-cream. My whole life flashed before me. It took just over a second – and nearly half of that was taken up with the 1963 school cross-country.

Bill Dawson and I stopped for a fag behind the science wing and Logger Goodwill saw us and told Mister Banks and we both got the cane and we had to do the whole course again by ourselves in the rain and Susan Crosby saw me and laughed and that was the worst bit because I really fancied her but in the end she got off with Logger Goodwill although I never knew what she saw in him because he was as ugly as a frog. Life, eh? Who needs it?

Anyway. The vivisectionist told me I should stop diving right away, but if I were stupid enough to persist in a hobby that was bound to kill me in the end I should certainly go no deeper than 10m.

Now a 10m dive in British waters, as you know, is like wrestling, blindfold, in a bath of freezing tagliatelle. You're more likely to meet intelligent life on Pluto than you are to stumble upon a solitary, geriatric periwinkle in 10m off Swanage pier.

"Listen," I demanded. "Are you absolutely sure I've got this … this UFO thing?"

"Absolutely one hundred per cent positive," he replied, with grim satisfaction.

"Can I have a second opinion?"

"Sure. You're fine."

I was desperate. "Have you any idea what this means to me? Never being able to dive again? I mean, it's my life we're talking here. Imagine how you'd feel if I said you could never practise medicine again."

"I'd be delighted," he replied. "I never wanted to be a doctor in the first place. Father pushed me into it. I wanted to dance, but he wouldn't hear of it. Oh no, that wasn't 'man's work'. He never really understood me, of course – not like Mother…"

He didn't even notice as I slipped out of the surgery and stumbled into the street, broken and blinded by tears.

What was to become of me? Was this the end? Would I ever again breathe the heady incense of salt spray and damp neoprene that is as oxygen itself to us diving folk?

PERHAPS open-heart surgery was the answer. It couldn't be so very difficult – like plumbing, really, with wobbly bits. Perhaps I could do it myself. A mirror, a half-decent bone saw…

Anyway, one thing was certain. I wasn't going to spend the rest of my days as an outcast, gazing down on the world I loved from 10m. I needed to consult another doctor. Preferably one that wasn't a dangerously deluded psychopath whose sole, frustrated ambition was to dance at Covent Garden with the Sugar Plum Fairies.

That was how I got to see Dr Peter Wilmshurst, Official Medicine Man of the British Sub-Aqua Club and Head of Everything at St Thomas' Hospital in London.

Due to Health Service cuts, Peter was the only doctor left there. We climbed the rusty, iron fire ladder to his office, a converted bed-pan storage closet on the seventeenth floor.

I glanced in on the old wards, now air-conditioned office suites of the Administration Department, most attractively conceived by Nico of Knightsbridge. I was particularly struck by the droll use of *trompe-l'œil*, drawing one's attention inexorably towards the Hockney pool scene where once, back in the quaint old days of public funding, the Special Baby Care Unit had been.

Once installed in Wilmshurst's office, he lit a candle and motioned me to sit on the bench he had improvised from bound editions of *Obstetrics & Double Entry Bookkeeping*.

He handed me a cold coffee in a urine sample flask and turned on that legendary bedside charm.

"Which purely imaginary disease are you going to whine about today?" he asked. "You'd better make it snappy – I've got a suspected necrotising fascilitis downstairs. If you don't look lively, there won't be enough of him left to treat."

"I've got a hole in the heart. It's making me depressed. They say I can't dive."

"Dive? Hah! I'm surprised you can walk, frankly. A PFO is an extremely serious condition. It's almost always fatal. Few sufferers have survived beyond 95."

"But... I...."

"Had any toe problems?"

You could have knocked me over with a feather star. I gasped: "Why, how on earth did you know?"

"I have highly developed psychic powers. In fact, I'm Chairman of the Society for the Investigation of Paranormal Phenomena, and in that capacity I have taken part in many scientifically validated experiments.

"These have proved beyond all reasonable doubt that certain individuals can reverse the normal chronology we know as 'linear causality', thereby seeming to predict the future.

"Of course, in reality, the linear nature of time is merely a convention invoked by humans to simplify our everyday existence.

We psychics prefer to think of time as circular, or even spherical. We have the ability, if you like, to cross the circle from any point to any other, whereas most people are condemned to circumnavigate the circumference.

"Besides, your foot's in plaster and you're on crutches."

I was impressed, I can tell you. In a medical world illuminated by technological triumphs like microsurgery and the body scanner, we are in danger of undervaluing the simple intuition of the born doctor.

"Let's take a look," he suggested. "Ah. Just as I thought. It's a classical complex trauma-induced referred resonance injury."

I nodded slowly. "Yes. Privately, I have always suspected something along those lines. But I haven't got a bloody clue what it is."

Wilmshurst allowed himself his annual, faint suggestion of a smile.

"It's childishly obvious, really. You stub your toe. The shock waves are transmitted through the tibia, slightly displacing the patella, causing subsequent over-compensation in the lateral muscle groups, which leads to a corresponding weakening of the gluteus minima and a resulting, barely perceptible, displacement of the hip joint.

"This tilts the pelvis, creating torsion in the vertebrae of the lower lumbar region and prompting an exaggerated curvature of the upper spine, which typically causes excess wear of the cartilagineous pad between the neck vertebrae C5 and C6.

"A chronic pressure develops upon the nerve serving the digits of the right hand, which is usually relieved by a slight inclination of the head, reducing blood flow through the carotid artery to the frontal lobes of the brain and causing, classically, the symptoms of short-term memory loss.

"Had any trouble of that sort?"

"What sort?" I enquired.

"Ah. Right. I see."

"Look, I can't hang around here all day chin-wagging. I've got a hospital appointment. Can you direct me to St Thomas'?"

Looking back, of course, my problem had been getting worse gradually for years – but so slowly that I'd never really noticed the change in my behaviour.

On one occasion, for instance, I'd forgotten to take my fins from my dive bag, which I'd left in the car, and I couldn't get them because I'd left the keys to the car in the van. That shouldn't have been a problem because I also had the keys to the van, but I'd left them in the cubby-hole on the boat and I'd forgotten to get the boat keys back from Ted.

Ted was supposed to be looking after the boat keys while I dived, which I couldn't do because I'd forgotten to get my fins from my dive bag (which, you will recall, I'd forgotten to take out of the car). And Ted was on the other boat. Which, as it turned out, he couldn't start because its keys were in the van.

Nobody in the Branch seemed to find my behaviour in any way worrying – even though we were on an explosives course at the time. In fact, shortly after that particular episode they elected me Diving Officer.

And after 15 years in the BSAC, I have to agree, I was ideally qualified for the job.

The kittie –
a study in duality

IF I'VE LEARNED anything in my 20 years as pastry chef, international crime boss and Carmelite nun, it's this: that there are only two kinds of people. There are the ones who turn up at the dive site with enough equipment to raise the *Titanic*, and those who gaily board the hardboat with a glove, odd fins and a pork pie.

It's hard to know which is more dangerous. On the face of it, the *kittie* would seem to be a model of common sense and responsibility. After all, he's allowed for every conceivable eventuality.

"This?" he will smugly reply to your puzzled enquiry. "This is your Maelstrom Mark IV Bi-Metal Nucleic Nitrometer. It automatically calculates the spontaneous magnetic deviation resulting from intermittent sun spot activity by taking a bearing on Alpha Centauri (Earth's nearest astral neighbour) and resolving it against the radio signal transmitted by the atomic clock at Greenwich Observatory. I had to send off to NASA for it. Believe it or not, you can still only get the Mark III in Europe. Sometimes I despair, I really do."

However, in a big swell, the sheer weight of the devoted kittie can affect the sea-worthiness of even the most robust dive boat. It's as if John Bantin had hung on to every piece of equipment he'd ever been asked to test, and attached it to his body with a karabiner clip.

I've dived with a buddy who carried more knives than a Millwall supporters' coach – who sported more torches than the night shift at the Ku Klux Klan – whose octopus rig resembled that molecular model of polytetrafluorethylene in the Open University advanced science module.

But did it make him a better diver? Don't you find yourself wondering why someone should need all that mechanical reassurance before he feels safe enough to get in the water?

Mind you, in this particular instance, I had reason to be grateful for my partner's kit fetish. I'd left my wetsuit at the dry cleaners (or was it the other way round) and the day might have been a complete write-off if Arnold hadn't been carrying a spare in a special pouch that doubled as lifting bag, SMB and emergency inflatable boat with water distillation unit and full satellite navigation capability.

For reasons of safety, Arnold doubled up on everything. Two cylinders (the second not so much a pony as a dray horse), each with a matching pair of octopus rigs. Fins on his hands as well as his feet, two masks (one on the back of his head), a full range of breathing media (air, nitrox, hydrox, dettox, krypton-argonox and pure, unadulterated bollox).

As well as the conventional goody bag, he carried a baddy bag.

I was never sure whether his dive knife was such a good idea – it was a double-edged sword.

He wore two watches, one set to the right time and one to the wrong time. If the right one were to go wrong, at least there was a chance that the wrong one would be right.

His inflexible insistence on carrying a duplicate weight belt nearly cost him his life on several occasions – notably on the famous Wall in the Cayman Islands, where he reached a depth of 5000 feet before he could ram enough air into his twin stab jackets to reverse his descent.

Then there was his photographic gear. Terrified in case he missed a shot through equipment failure, he always carried a second camera that automatically took a picture of his first camera as it took a picture of the subject. Or should I say subjects, for he would only photograph pairs of creatures, in case one of them didn't come out.

If I gave the impression that Arnold and I dived as a pair, then I have misled you: it was a cardinal rule of Arnold's that he dived with two buddies. "Then," he would cheerfully explain, "if I lose one, I can always continue the dive with my spare. It's just common sense, is that."

As you might imagine, the beaches of the South Coast were not awash with hordes of eager volunteers queuing up to dive with Arnold. Eventually, he resigned from the two Branches of which he was a member, bought a twin-engined catamaran and emigrated to New Zealand.

Over a drink in the Two Brewers, he explained that he had always admired the Kiwis for retaining control of both North and South islands. He winked knowingly at me. "My kind of people," he said.

Strangely enough, I missed him. Strangely, because I am his exact opposite in every respect. I am his antithesis incarnate. Where Arnold insisted on two of everything, it's quite unusual if I manage to muster one.

Last time the Branch dived in Cornwall, I spent the first three days scouring car-boot sales for items of equipment – or at least items that with a little ingenuity might be converted into equipment. Necessity is indeed the mother of invention.

I discovered that the U-bend from a bathroom sink makes a formidable snorkel. Leave in place the little circular grill at the top, and it filters out that disgusting mat of human hair, soap and dental floss one usually inhales while snorkelling in the Channel.

A pair of preserving jars, complete with seals, make a perfectly adequate mask – although the magnifying effects of the glass take a little getting used to. I fainted with fright when I was attacked by the 60ft brittle star.

I won't bore you with the old "dive computer scam", cobbling together the Game Boy and the Lambretta rev counter. Or the oldest trick in the book: how to make a perfectly serviceable 85-litre cylinder out of a 1955 Electrolux vacuum cleaner, a pair of braces and a garden hose. Let's own up – we've all done it at one time or another.

Suffice it to say that diving teaches you the single most important lesson that life has to offer: it takes all sorts.

It just ain't like it was

JANUARY again. My forty-third, and my fourteenth as a diver. Cause enough for a moment's quiet contemplation as I stand here on Swanage Pier, watching the seagulls trying in vain to break the ice in the bay.

So much has changed. And yet so little. Yesterday, we dived from the 2.5m Zodiac we called Geronimo (because it was *a patchy* old wreck). Today we dive from the jet-propelled, twin-hulled supercruiser we have to moor in the deep-water harbour at Milford Haven.

Yet Arthur 'The Laughing Policeman' Muldoon is still the social secretary, nobody has yet successfully identified the marks for the *James Eagan Layne*, and the beer at the Cat & Hacksaw still tastes like samples taken at a special clinic for dromedaries.

Why, it's hard to believe it was nearly five years ago that Tonker Tollesby threw up over Mike Todd's solid gold presentation Siebe Gorman hard-hat in front of the Prince of Wales.

Or that a decade has passed since Colin 'Mental' Mungo dived to 80m in Grymmpike Black Tarn at midnight, wearing only Wellingtons and a red satin basque. (Actually, come to think of it, that wasn't 10 years ago at all. It was last Tuesday. Funny how the memory can play tricks on you.)

Among the more significant developments of recent years has been the reduction in the size of wetsuits.

When I first started diving, your wetsuit was close fitting, certainly, but not excessively so. The fit could be described as snug, but never mean. Today, sadly, all that has changed. In tune with the times, corners have been cut, pennies pinched, ships spoiled for ha'pennyworths of tar.

Your contemporary suit might cost a month's salary and look like an explosion in a paint factory, but it is apt to squeeze most unpleasantly around a fellow's midriff, to rudely bully the hind quarters, and, most eye-wateringly of all, to grab at those most tender articles of the male anatomy and to wring them in an excruciating, vicelike fashion.

The same tendency to meanness seems to have afflicted the aqualung, too. Why, time was when a chap would pop up from a decent dive with a clear 100 atmospheres of air in his bottle. Nowadays, as often as not, it's all gone in half an hour.

Also, I'm all for giving youngsters the chance to do their bit about the branch, but in my opinion we're asking for trouble when we allow mere children to instruct.

To teach someone to dive competently and safely requires the kind of maturity that only comes with age and experience. Yet – I cannot tell a lie – in my very own Sturminster Branch, I have seen so-called instructors who simply cannot be a day over 30.

I mention no names, and I'm sure the same sort of thing is going on at branches all over the country. But I'm sorry, I can't help it; just because a dangerous practice is popular, doesn't make it safe.

I could go on. For example, I wonder if you've noticed how much heavier boat engines are nowadays? It's quite clearly a conspiracy.

Little by little, the manufacturers have added an ounce here and an ounce there, to make some paltry saving or other. They've done it slyly and on the quiet, over the years, thinking nobody would notice.

Well, they reckoned without sharp-eyed, shrewd old seadogs like Andy Blackford. They can consider the whistle well and truly blown.

It wouldn't have happened in my time, of course, not when your outboard motor gloried in the name of the British Seagull and was "Empire made".

Now, of course, the British Seagull has perished in the oilspill of history, the empire ends at Camber Sands, and the Japs have smiled and bowed their way on to the transom of every boat in Christendom.

Damned tragedy.

Here's another thing: this "global warming" nonsense. Pshaw! Fiddlesticks! As is plainly obvious to anyone who's been around as long as I have, the sea is very markedly colder than it used to be.

In fact, this development prompted a New Year's resolution; namely, to dig out my old drysuit for the forthcoming season. "Dig out" proved uncomfortably near the truth. I finally found it in the garden, where it had seen three years' service keeping the starlings off the raspberries.

I was compelled to buy a new one. It cost me more than my first motor car, and to add insult to injury it was no less mean and skimpy than the aforementioned wetsuit and cylinder.

"Young lady!" I called in a strangled voice from the changing room. "This won't do. The seal is far too tight beneath my chin."

"Which chin would that be, Mister Blackford?" replied the cheeky young minx. Of course, this is what you get when you employ mere adolescents in responsible positions. If she was 35, I'm the Queen Mother.

If only it were just the suits and the cylinders that have shrunk in the last 14 years. But it's the whole planet.

When I learned to dive, Eilat was an exotic dream-destination. Soldiers with Ouzis rode shotgun on the bus that droned down through the desert from Tel Aviv, spiriting me away to dive in a fantastic submarine Eden that began 1m offshore.

But last week at the Cat & Hacksaw, I overheard one acned whippersnapper telling another over a half of shandy, "Nah, forget the bleedin' Caymans, mate, it's a bleedin' nonsense. You wanna go to Sipidan. It's nice, is Sipidan."

You've got to make allowances, of course; they were young and perhaps they didn't know any better. I know it's hard to tell these days, but I'd be amazed if either of them was a day over 40.

The wreck of the Wigan Trolley

UNDER NORMAL circumstances, this article would have been around 1000 words long. But it's a mere 935. That's the Recession for you. Everything is being surreptitiously cut back, eroded, down-graded, gnawed-away-at.

It's affecting every aspect of life. My hairdresser complained to me only yesterday that business is terrible. Either people are saving money by having fewer haircuts, he said, or the national rate of hair growth is slowing down.

Personally, I favour the latter explanation. In fact, a spokesman from the National Federation Of Hairdressers' Econometrics & Statistical Projections Unit predicted gloomily that hair was likely to "enter a period of negative growth, in line with an overall shrinkage in the manufacturing sector". By the final quarter, he added, "the unthinkable and terrifying might well be a reality, with hair actually getting shorter by the day, finally vanishing altogether down the nation's follicles".

Nor is diving immune from the effects of economic Recession. Because I'm a world-renowned author and intellectual giant, I am constantly offered huge financial inducements to sample diving holidays in far-flung, exotic locations. It's dirty work, but someone's got to do it.

Why, only last year, the President of Kenya engaged in an ugly public dispute with His Most Marvellousness The Prince Umbo Monolulu, Grand High Chief Extraordinary, Most Fundamental Emissary Of The Great Walrus Father, Protector Of Foam And Cloud, Wearer Of The Big Blue Watch and Lord Lieutenant Of The Wayward Islands, both claiming that I had accepted their invitations to spend the May Bank Holiday assessing their best sites for DIVER.

This year, on the other hand, I was forced to choose between Runswick Frog Ponds (a flooded guano pit near Mexborough) and a site of historical interest on the Manchester Ship Canal, where archaeologists working under Dame Margaret Rule had stumbled on the fossilised remains of a Sainsbury's trolley of the Late Jurassic period.

After much agonising, I threw in my lot with Dame Margaret.

It is hard to convey the mood of electric anticipation that pervaded our party as, inch by inch, we exposed The Wigan Trolley.

The Great Woman explained the full significance of the find to the world's media, whose representatives, held back only by a line of burly policemen, threatened to engulf the site. The Trolley, she announced, was far more than a mere castor-mounted supermarket basket.

It was, in fact, a "time capsule", miraculously preserved across the centuries in a compress of dead cats and old mattresses, which would tell us more about life in prehistoric Lancashire than any number of old George Formby songs.

Can words adequately express the emotion of the moment as my air lift spirited away the last ounce of silt to reveal a packet of alphabet soup – soup from a time when some remote ancestor of Kendall McDonald first crawled from its stagnant lake to draw first breath upon a rotting log?

Wigan Soup, of course, was soon to become the most baffling anthropological enigma since Piltdown Man. The alphabet, apparently, bore no relation to any known script. The most advanced computer techniques were applied in an attempt to break the code, but to no avail.

Despite the combined efforts of the world's most respected lexicographers and semanticists, it was I who finally cracked it. I spread the letters out on a sheet in an entirely arbitrary order – and recognised them immediately as one of Dr Peter Wilmshurst's medical articles.

While I was offered the Oxford Chair of Comparative Etymology for my services to linguistics, it was only luck, really. I could just as easily have dismissed that pattern of letters, like everyone else, as a randomised jumble of incomprehensible

characters, devoid of any intelligible sense or meaning.

Meanwhile, back at the dive site, things were hotting up. Every relic we retrieved from the hold of The Wigan Trolley cast new light upon our primitive Lancastrian forebears.

On the basis of the first day's finds, it would seem that Wigan Man subsisted on a diet of pies, Capstan Full Strength and, interestingly, concentrated bleach.

Which suggests that we're more like our ancestors than we thought – and more unlike them, too. After all, most modern Liverpudlians smoke Capstan Full Strength and drink bleach. Few eat pies.

After a week in the Ship Canal, I was cold as a Christmas card from Sadam Hussein. In the great skinflint tradition of London Branch, I had built my own drysuit from two goody bags and an old pea colander, and I was regretting it.

Emptying the suit after a particularly difficult shift on the rear left castor assemblage, I disgorged a Three-Toed Newt, a copy of *Scouting For Boys* with a foreword by Julian Clary and a cheque, signed *Bernard Eaton* which is currently touring the Americas as part of the British Museum's Wonders Of The World exhibition.

But I digress. As I said, I was cold. I yearned for the clear, tepid waters of an idyllic lagoon, where even an aqualung seems a needless encumbrance.

Wincing as I tore rusting bed springs from between my toes with Dame Margaret's 17th century, silver-filigree monkey wrench, I was overwhelmed with nostalgia. I longed for those pre-Recessionary days when a dive offered the possibility, however faint, of encountering a fish. Or at least a sponge. Or anything.

Two or three Intercontinental Ballistic Facsimiles later, and I was in business. Prince Monolulu's right-hand honcho, it was, who came up with the goods:

"Hail O Andy-Blackford-Sahib, whose Pungent Manliness exceeds even that of the Brown Goats upon the Island known as Roger, and whose Magic enables him to slip beneath the waves like a discarded Double Diamond bottle.

"It will be to the Eternal Honour of His Fantasticness and his 200 Undulating Wives if you would join him without delay on the island of Tesco for a week of wild and uninhibited excess. Please bring your...

(As a result of recessionary pressures, this article has been prematurely curtailed. We apologise for any inconvenience. *The Publisher.*)

From the cold
to the chilli

IT WAS IN 1984 that I dedicated my life to diving; that I devoted myself to enabling others to appreciate the secret mysteries of our planet and, in so doing, perchance to discover themselves.

I remember as if it were yesterday the exact moment at which my hobby became my burning preoccupation.

I was at my desk at Bollum, Smigma, Gnat & Margerino, the advertising agency where I worked as a copywriter.

I was involved in a protracted wrangle with Simon Tharston-Swinge, aristocratic Adonis, Cambridge rowing blue, agency heart-throb and absolute lamebrain, over the lyrics of a jingle I had written for Spankie's Famous Mutton Scratchings.

Spankie lambs are yummy lambs
Spankie lambs are scrummy
Spankie lambs taste just as good
For only half the money

"Hey, I mean Andy, it's fabulous. Nobody's saying it's not fabulous. It's an award winner, no doubt about that. It's just that it's… illegal."

"Illegal."

"Yah. Apparently, you can't say that Spankie's are 'only half the money' unless you stipulate exactly what they're only half the money of."

"How about something twice as expensive?"

"Also, 'just as good' is a subjective value judgement, apparently, and pretty insupportable as a generalisation."

"Yes, but…"

"Also, apparently, even if you could identify a more expensive competitor, it might not always be true. Prices vary from shop to shop, seemingly."

"I see, but…"

"Anyway, worry not. I've solved the problem."

"Tell me."

"OK. Well read this."

Spankie lambs are yummy lambs

Spankie lambs are nice

Spankie lambs taste virtually identical (according to a panel of independent experts)

For approximately half the recommended retail price (subject to regional variations)

My leaving party was held at the Proctor & Gamble in Lever Street. I'm told it went well. At the time I was signing up as an instructor at Aquapulco, a dive shop and training school in the largely forgotten Mexican resort of Qaxaxaxxalaxa.

Its proprietor was Bengt, a Swedish-Aztec schizophrenic with a face like the Sea of Tranquillity and the generosity of a pickled stoat testicle. I grew to love him as a brother. In exactly the same way, in fact, as Cain loved Abel.

When I turned up for work on my first day, he seemed vague and distracted.

"Ees OK. I lose something, ess all."

"Perhaps I can help?" I offered. "What have you lost?"

"Three divers," he replied casually. He waved in the general direction of the Gulf of Mexico. "Over there. Las' night."

I was horrified.

"Oh my God! At what time last night?"

"Don' ask me. I was drunk." Then, "Hey! Don' worry, Gringo. We find 'em on Shark Island. Everytheeng roun' here, she end up on Shark Island."

As it turned out, he was right. He set about their rescue with the usual Mexican sense of urgency. By the time the hapless divers were finally airlifted off the island, there were four of them.

Two of them had married, eaten the third and produced two children.

The eldest child had completed a correspondence course in Information Technology from a college in Louisiana, conducted entirely through messages in bottles.

Armed with his new knowledge, he built a primitive radio

transmitter out of conch shells and began to broadcast Mayday messages around the clock.

However, because of freak atmospheric conditions in the Van Allen Belt, the signals were deflected and could be received only in the remote, northern Siberian city of Zstring – and even here, only upon the dental bridgework of Zortan Wildeyes, a mystic and religious zealot who assumed the distress signal to be a direct and personal communication from the god Norg.

He interpreted the signals as an incitement to launch the Crusade of Blood and Fire, and with his acolytes he swept through the Steppes, spreading the gospel of Norg and harassing the indigenous ptarmigan which, according to the Norgites, are "the Devil's wildfowl".

Meanwhile, I was back in Qaxaxaxxalaxa with Bengt, devoting myself to enabling others to appreciate the secret mysteries, etc. It wasn't proving easy. Others, it seemed, were not as interested in appreciating mysteries as they were in trying to drown themselves and, where possible, me.

I'd always envied the rugged diving instructor with the permatan and the wake of simpering, bikini-clad beauties. But the reality was depressingly different.

My first pupil was a German businessman. He weighed 146kg and was about as much fun as the Ian Paisley *Bumper Book of After-Dinner Jokes*.

The very act of breathing made him out of breath. On land, he resembled a plastic sack of jellied eels. In water, he moved with the same speed and grace as the Isle of Wight.

The first time he entered the water, I half expected the Queen to break a bottle of champagne over him. The Gulf rose by a metre and low-lying coastal regions of Texas suffered calamitous flooding.

This caused a major diplomatic incident between the respective governments of Germany and the USA, and the UN Security Council sat for two nights in extraordinary session in an attempt to avert armed conflict.

Happily, the issue was defused when Heidelberg ritually dissolved its twinning arrangement with Disneyworld.

Meanwhile, my German broke the world air consumption record by exhausting his twin-set after seven minutes' finning on the surface. The cylinders collapsed like beer cans with his final breath.

He switched to his snorkel but it melted in the stupendous heat generated by the friction of air on propylene. In the end, an ocean-going tug towed him out to sea where, as the centrepiece of a Honduran military exercise, he was sunk by naval gunfire.

Not an ideal beginning to my career as a diving instructor, I reflected that evening over a pint of lizard wine in the bar of the Dead Horse.

Still, things could only look up.

I HAVE never worked so hard as I did during that next year. Looking back, I can recall only an indistinct blur – a sort of frantic dream, in which interminable periods in the water and the lecture room were punctuated by mad spells in the Dead Horse with my boss, the unspeakable Bengt, drinking tequila.

A word about this most singular spirit. Distilled by Bengt himself in the radiator of our compressor engine, its principle ingredient was the fermented juice of the mescal cactus, a spiny, unexceptional-looking vegetable that nevertheless had the power to stir up the murkiest deeps of the subconscious mind, and to liberate the howling monsters that lurk therein.

It was not unusual, after four or five polythene boat balers of this terrible stuff, to find oneself running through the streets of Babylon or Nagasaki, clad only in a pair of puce snake-skin pyjamas, pursued by a horrifying hybrid of giant scorpion and Mrs McManus, who saw me stealing Milky Bars from the corner shop in Roman Road, Middlesbrough, when I was five.

The hangover induced by an excess of this home-grown liquor defies description.

As far as my teaching went, I suppose I was learning my trade. It was an odd sort of clientele who signed up with Aquapulco, largely because the name of Qaxaxaxxalaxa was too long, and the place itself too short, for inclusion on most maps of Mexico.

Nor was its claim to the status of a Proper Place helped by its relations with the Church. These had been decidedly shaky ever since Bengt had sold off, bit by bit, the mummified remains of a local saint, Santa Donna Assunta Consuela de los Angeles de la

Conceptione, as pork scratchings in the smoking lounge of the Dead Horse.

Consequently it was a special kind of person who pitched up at the diving school with a pair of fins, a glazed smile and $20 (or the equivalent in small livestock). Had my pupils ever formed a queue, you might have been excused for supposing them to be hopeful actors, waiting for bit parts in a film by Frederico Fellini.

During one season, I trained an Icelandic fire eater, a pair of exotic dancers from Islamabad (joined at the hip), a Maidenhead estate agent, the entire entourage of King Mamoud the Unreasonable, pretender to the throne of Senegal, and the variety act known as Alberto Wilcocks and his Rumba Racoons.

I can claim, with some pride, that apart from the regrettable loss of a racoon on the wreck of the *Pope Leo XXXIV*, my Novice Diver courses were conducted without serious incident and to the complete satisfaction of all concerned.

I only wish the same could be said of Bengt's record as an Advanced Instructor. His training methods were, at best, highly personal. He scorned the computer, relying instead upon a battered and tequila-stained 1949 edition of the Mexican Airforce Decompression Tables.

These were extremely liberal, being based upon the nitrogen absorbency characteristics of four types of igneous rock, and permitted the diver to remain at more or less any depth he wished, for as long as his air held out.

Indeed, so many divers had disappeared during the futile, week-long struggles against the immutable mainstays of human physiology that were Bengt's diving courses, that Aquapulco had become the first port of call of the Missing Persons' Bureau in Mexico City.

I came to know their two most senior agents well. Almost every Friday, their rust-eaten Cadillac Eldorado would bounce along the dusty track to the dive school. Once they had established that the solutions to at least half a dozen of their unsolved cases were to be found in Bengt's guest register, they would relax and play Cluedo through the night with us, drinking tequila and sexually harassing Florentina, the smoulderingly beautiful barmaid and part-time rat-catcher.

I once accompanied Bengt as he took six novices on a training dive in El Fandango Negro, a vicious and unpredictable whirlpool in which, only last year, had vanished the *Exxon Valdez II*, a 100,000-tonne supertanker. The loss of this giant ship would, in itself, have been ample testimony to the sheer might of the Fandango. Eerily, though, the *Exxon* surfaced three months later in the South China Sea, completely undamaged yet affording no clue as to the whereabouts of the crew.

As a matter of course, Lloyd's sent a team to Aquapulco, but even Bengt's books could not account for the 98 missing seamen.

That Bengt should regard El Fandango Negro as a suitable dive for six complete novices, including an octogenarian greatgrandmother in post-operative therapy following a double hip replacement, says more about his teaching technique than words ever can.

At the pre-dive briefing, his words were almost drowned by the terrifying roar of the Fandango's vortex.

"Now looky! Lissen up good, 'cos I say zees only once. Mebbe not even once, OK?

"El Fandango, he is a bastardo, savee? Eef he's speening, he pull you down, crush your bone, tear your flesh to meencemeat, an' speet you out. That's eef he's speening.

"But every hour, for six minutes," continued Bengt, emphasising the point by holding up eight fingers, "he stop speening. Six minutes. Only trouble ees, I dunno which six minutes. So we might as well dive right now, OK? Kit up."

On that occasion, we were lucky. But Bengt was not always so lucky. Or rather, his divers weren't, for Bengt seemed to be protected by some invisible, demonic guardian. In all the time I knew him, he never so much as broke a fingernail.

Dive training – the Postlethwaite way

DIVERS AREN'T what they used to be. In my day, men were men and women, by and large, were men, too. The course was tough – you were three years in the shallow end of the pool before they let you within a mile of a snorkel. You had to tread water for two days, holding an outboard above your head. To pass your life-saving, you had to drown yourself, just so you knew what it was like.

Also, your modern diving instructor is a pussy cat. In the good old days, when a wetsuit was just that – a *wet* suit – your instructor was an overbearing, humourless, insensitive, bullying, sadistic bigot.

Mine was the grandaddy of them all. He's retired now – works part time as a pit prop near Doncaster. But I'll never forget his first lecture, that wild January night in the flooded Nissen hut on Grimm Fell…

"Hello. I'm yer diving instructor. The name's Bill, but you can call me Mister Postlethwaite. Is that your mask, son? It is? Then you're even dafter than you look. Take my advice – stick it in your back garden. Bit o' pond weed, couple of newts. Make a nice little feature, will that.

"Right, then. Divin'. Rule One: divin' is a mug's game. It's very, very dangerous. In fact, it's very often fatal.

"If someone tells you he's been divin' regularly for ten years and he's still alive, he's lyin'. Either he's lyin' about how long he's been divin', or he's lyin' about bein' alive.

"Either way, it's bloody well dangerous and stupid and it'll end in tears.

"So that's that. You have been warned. And if you end up cold and blue on the slab with yer blood like dandelion an' burdock, don't go blamin' me.

"OK. Divin' kit. This here's a wetsuit. Do try an' get the correct size. If it's too big, it'll let in water and you'll get Eye-po-thermia.

"Eye-po-thermia makes you stupid – or in your case, son, more stupid – and if you don't die of cold, you'll do somethin' stupid and that'll kill yer.

"On the other 'and, if it's too small, it'll cut off the flow of blood to your extremities – no laughin' at the back – and you'll get... what? Hands up! Right! Eye-po-thermia.

"This is a drysuit. Dodgy, are these. I knew a bloke once, his valve stuck an' he shot up from 30m like a cross between Fatty Arbuckle an' a Trident missile. They found 'im four miles inland. Well, some of 'im, anyroad.

"This is a dive computer. Absolutely bloody lethal. For all the good it'll do yer, it might as well be a Nintendo Gameboy.

"The only thing less reliable than a dive computer is yer divin' tables. Go down to the right depth for the wrong time, an' you're dead. Go down for the right time to the wrong depth and you're dead. Come up too fast an' yer innards turn t'frogspawn an' you're dead. Come up too slow an' you'll run out of air an' you're dead. Or else you'll get Eye-po-thermia. Suit yerself.

"There's lots of different kinds of divin' tables, an' they're all bloody useless. Personally, I prefer the Mexican Cavalry Tables, 'cos you can stay down all day if you want to, and nobody gives a monkey's.

"Next: the Gas Laws. The Gas Laws are the basis of divin'. There's a whole string of 'em – there's Boyle's Law, Burke's Law and Coleslaw. And the one you're bloody well bound to run into, first time you go divin' – Sod's Law.

"Basically, they all say the same thing: namely, the deeper you dive, the more likely you are to end up dead.

"This is a weightbelt. The weights are made of lead. Here we are – the race that put a man on the moon – an' we can't come up with something lighter than lead. Still, soldier on.

"The weightbelt is an ironical sort of item: if it's heavy, you'll sink, the Gas Laws'll get yer an' you're dead. If it's light, you'll come up too fast and you'll get a Bend.

"A Bend is short for Decompression Sickness. There's lots o' different types of Decompression Sickness. The nicest type is called Subcutaneous Emphysema, which is Greek for Horrible Agony. I won't bother you with the other types, 'cos if you get 'em, you're dead.

"Any questions so far?

"Right, well that's the good news. Next: Nitrogen Narcosis. This is caused by divin' too deep. Too deep can be anythin' from 80m to sittin' in a boat on the surface. It all depends on who it is. An' you won't know if it's you until it's too late.

"Nitrogen Narcosis makes you even more stupid than Eye-po-thermia. A bloke I knew got Nitrogen Narcosis and he thought he was a fish. He dumped his aqualung, swallowed a mackerel fly and ended up bein' served with chips an' mushy peas at a Rotary Club supper in Scarborough.

"Right. When we dive, we observe the Buddy System. This is an extremely important procedure, designed to create the illusion of Safety In Numbers. It works like this: on the boat, before you dive, your buddy shows you his kit, explainin' in great detail how each bit would work in an emergency – and you nod a lot and look serious an' pretend you're listenin'. Then later, underwater, when your buddy has an emergency, you back off to a safe distance and keep a careful eye on 'im 'til he's sorted it out.

"If by a stroke of bad luck, the emergency happens to you, the Buddy System still applies. Your buddy has air and, very probably, you don't. You approach your buddy quickly, preferably from behind, and transfer his demand valve from his mouth to yours, thus enabling you to breathe.

"Got that? Right. Kit up an' I'll see you in the quarry as soon as you've broken the ice and the wind drops to Force 7.

"Class dismissed."

The long road to Bovisand Harbour

IT WAS midnight of 31 August, 2020, when we joined the queue of boats waiting to be launched from Bovisand harbour. So far, we were making good time. We were still on the M25 – but at least we'd got as far as the Leatherhead exit.

Way over on the hard shoulder, I could just make out Bromley Branch's big, semi-inflatable, decommissioned Trident nuclear submarine. Why, it must be nearly two years since they'd broken down, on their way to Swanage. Still, they'd made the best of a bad job – built up quite a little community there, on the roadside.

There was a handful of neat little dwellings, ingeniously constructed from petrol cans and old stab jackets. There was even a school for the kids, in a hollowed-out copy of the BSAC diving manual.

They waved and shouted as we passed, and hurled brown ale bottles at us in their usual, cheerful way. I felt a sudden surge of affection for these tough, resourceful folk and resolved to give the RAC a gee-up when next an occasion arose.

Scanning the other 14 lanes of the clockwise carriageway, I realised that we divers were getting the best of things. The Windsurfers' Lane (number nine) was stationary and backed up right to the Dartford Tunnel and beyond.

At 3am, I handed over the wheel to our Equipment Officer. But try as he might, he couldn't get it back on the steering column. Still, it wasn't my problem. I'd driven my 24 hours, and I'd earned my rest.

I considered taking a sleeping tablet, but really I needed something stronger. So I opened my copy of DIVER and turned to the Great British Wrecks section, edited by Keswick Carlisle

McDonald, great-grandson of Kendall, later Lord McDonald of Hartlepool.

Back in the 20th century, the wrecks articles were never shorter than a double-page spread. But that was in the good old days, when there were ships, and they sank.

Now, of course, the vast majority of cargo is transported telekinetically, with a handful of clerks in a darkened room, thinking containers around the world at astonishing speeds. When these speeds exceed that of light itself, the cargo arrives at its destination before it leaves – an administrative nightmare for the customs people. On one occasion, four tons of eggs arrived in New York shortly before two thousand chickens left Southampton. The story was reported in the Press under the headline, "Which came first?"

Anyway, where was I? Ah, yes. The Great British Wreck.

Navigational aids are now so sophisticated that it is virtually impossible for a mariner to hit anything hard enough to sink his ship – even supposing there is a ship to sail, and a mariner to sail it, for world recession has long since put paid to the world's merchant fleets.

Imagine my excitement, then, when I turned to Great British Wrecks to discover, instead of the promised profile of Deric Ellerby (now 107), news of a genuine, old-style shipwreck!

"Divers," it read, "under the guidance of psychic and astrologer Ms Doris Stokes, have located the wreck of a small collier in 200m, 120 miles west of Land's End.

"The ship is thought to be the *Sir Bernard Eaton*, a 20th century tramp steamer out of Teddington, which sank in mysterious circumstances while bound for Paraguay with a priceless cargo of silver, gold and precious stones."

In a second, I was galvanised into action. I had to tell the rest of the lads about this. I grabbed the Branch VHF radio: LB 1, LB 1, LB 1, LB1, this is LB 2, come in please… (silence)… LB 1, LB1, LB2, come in please… (silence punctuated by deep, staccato noises, like a three-toed sloth on heat)… come in please, LB 1… (sudden, ear-splitting extract from Radio 4's 'Book At Bedtime': *The Idiot*, Dostoevsky's classic tale of love and gratuitous violence, adapted for radio by… more sloth noises)…

I gave up, as we always give up. At London Branch, as in

every other, we wear our radios in the same spirit as South Sea cannibal kings wear alarm clocks. They are a powerful ju-ju, they possess great, magical significance; for the wearer, they are a symbol of virility and potency. But as a means of communication, you might as well lug a tub of lard around with you.

To cut a long story short, two days later, we were launching the branch fusion-powered laser-navigated catamaran hydrofoil en route for the watery grave of the *Sir Bernard Eaton*.

We reached the dive site in a little under five minutes, and quickly kitted up.

Stepping gingerly on the bobbing heads of surfacing divers, we walked from the boat to the little blob buoy that marked "the spot".

As we sank beneath the waves, we were approached by a pretty girl, fetchingly dressed in a pink, shorty wetsuit and black stockings made from real fish nets.

"Official programme, sir?" she mouthed alluringly, and offered me a glossy A4 brochure entitled: "The Sir Bernard Eaton Experience – a mesmeric voyage of Exploration and Discovery".

I declined politely and continued my descent. At the 110m mark, I could just make out the shadowy shape of the wreck beneath me. But between me and it were 30 or so divers, some with children in push chairs. They appeared to be queuing outside a small, wooden shed.

As I approached, I saw that the shed was occupied by an elderly gentleman in the unmistakable livery of the Corps Of Commissionaires.

"How many's it for, guv?" he demanded. "Just yourself, is it? No nippers? Right. That'll be £50, thankin' you."

I was horrified. "You mean, I've got to pay to see the wreck?"

"Certainly, guv," he replied. "How else do you think we're goin' to pay for the restoration?"

"The what?"

"I mean, the bridge is lookin' decidedly dodgy. It's gonna cost six million quid to fix it, and the Government won't cough up. So pay up, mate, or make room for someone who will."

What can you say?

Eating divers is wrong

AS ALL devout readers of DIVER will recall, I visited the Bahamas recently in my capacity as Intrepid Roving Reporter.

It was only when I arrived in Nassau that the real purpose of the trip was revealed to me. I'd envisaged a relaxing week, lolling on coral beaches beneath swaying palms with dusky Bahamian maidens, their modesty preserved only by flimsy strings of beads and tiny shells.

I'd even agreed privately with myself that, given enough maidens and a sufficient shortage of beads, I might stay on indefinitely. My needs would have been humble enough – a grass hut by the ocean; an easel, perhaps; and a small distillery.

But life being what it is, life was having none of it. As it turned out, I was expected to report on a new shark dive: a priceless opportunity, they explained, to study these beautiful creatures at close quarters, free of such clumsy artificial distractions as protective suits, cages or bang sticks.

How nice, I replied. What an unexpected pleasure. How thoughtful of them to include me in their priceless opportunity.

The shark dive was in 20m of water on the edge of a sheer cliff which plummeted to the mind-numbing depths of some trench or other. The sharks lived in the trench, apparently, but it seems they'd happily climb the five miles or so to our ledge for a whiff of rotting fish entrails. I suppose that if you're a shark, there's not a lot of competition for your time.

1st shark: "What shall we do today, lads? Check out the chummy or cruise around, being menacing?"

2nd shark: "We was menacin' yesterday."

3rd shark: "And the day before. I spent the 'ole of Thursday

mornin' menacin' a sea cucumber. An' for what? I mean, where does it get yer, at the end of the day?"

2nd shark: "We don't 'ave to cruise around. There's no law sayin' we 'ave to cruise."

3rd shark: "You can't menace if you don't cruise. I mean, we're sharks, fer Gawd's sakes – restless predators of the deep – cold-hearted, gimlet-eyed, single-minded 'unters of the trackless wastes, ever-movin', our territory as wide an' deep as the ocean itself. Stop cruisin', and what are we? A bunch of soddin' great white elephants, sat there on the bottom, accumulatin' barnacles."

2nd shark: "True."

1st shark: "Right. It's the rottin' fish, then. Last one to the bucket's a blenny."

They slipped over the rim of the cliff like a squadron of stealth bombers, sleek, purposeful and tense with tight-coiled power.

We crouched motionless behind coral heads, mouths dry, eyes wide. The beating of my heart, it later turned out, was picked up at the Woods Hole Oceanographic Institute and triggered a full-scale national alert.

One by one, they swept over our bucket of chum. A barely perceptible twitch of the tail was enough to send them streaking smoothly away over the brink.

2nd shark: "Same old rubbish. Fish guts à la Stagnant Blood, followed by Fricassee of Fetid Fin."

3rd shark: "Bloody cheapskates. 'Ere, 'ow much do you think they charge for this divin' experience of a lifetime?"

2nd shark: "Thirty quid, I 'eard."

3rd shark: "Thirty smackers. Marvellous, innit? Let's see, that's thirty times ten, that's three 'undred quid. Blimey, we should be on smoked salmon an' caviar for that."

2nd shark: "It's exploitation, that's what it is. You can just imagine it, can't you: 'What shall we give the sharks today, Bill? Rack o' lamb spiced wiv rosemary an' a selection of fresh vegetables? Nah – too much 'assle. Give 'em rottin' fish 'eads again – they won't know the bleedin' difference.'"

3rd shark: "I've got a good mind to bite their bleedin' legs off."

2nd shark: "I'm with you there, brother. Down wiv the exploitatin' capitalist oppressors! Try *this* for the divin' experience of a lifetime, matey!"

1st shark: "Hey, steady on, lads, steady on! Let's just get this in perspective. We bite their legs off, and what happens? End of shark dive. End of free meal ticket. I mean, it might only be rotting fish, but I know certain sharks who'd give their dorsal fins for rotting fish."

3rd shark: "Yeah, he's right. I remember when I was a kid, we used to dream of a bucket of fish guts. Bloody luxury, was fish guts."

1st shark: "Precisely my point. Everything's relative. I mean, remember when I got that part in *Jaws*? I had to laugh: there I was, a film star, and all I had to eat in six weeks was three barrels, an aqualung and Robert Shaw."

2nd shark: "Hah! Listen to 'im! Has it never occurred to you, that's exactly what they want you to think? Oh, yeah, toss 'em any old crap – they'll be so bleedin' grateful they'll come back again tomorrow! You are nothin' but a prawn, my friend – a prawn in the capitalists' game. A dupe, a mug, a patsy. I mean, where would we be if our glorious forebears had thought the same way as you do? Precisely! Doin' 5000 laps a day of some goldfish bowl in

Marineland for the titillation of arthritic octogenarians. Well, you can count me out, pal."

3rd shark: "Me, too. He's right, Darren. We're sharks. We eat people. It is written. It is our destiny. So we might as well be true to ourselves – startin' now, with that big bloke at the end with the tatty kit."

2nd shark: "What, the one tryin' to 'ide behind the sea urchin? Bit down at 'eel? Looks like a Brit?"

1st shark: "Boys, boys! Before you do anything rash, please hear me out. I have one thing only to say, and it's this: I wash my hands entirely of the whole business. If you want me, I'll be down on level 98, doing a spot of menacing. *Au revoir*."

It was at this point that I broke ranks and struck out strongly (some might say "fled") for the surface.

Over the next 50 or so episodes of *Last Gasp*, I shall be exploring the subject of "Basic Finning Techniques in the Pool".

A tale of sugar, Santa and Zambonga

IT'S OVER for another 11 months. "Allelujah" is what I say. Sometimes I think Life is just 70 Christmases, linked together by periods of ever-increasing angst, panic and neurosis which attain their nerve-frazzling climax in those final nanoseconds of shopping time, as Lillywhites' security guard shoulders shut the doors on 24 December.

It's ironic. Nowadays, we're forced into a state resembling Christian grace by a potent cocktail of guilt and commercial pressure. We're so terrified in case we haven't overspent enough, or that we might be seen as thoughtless or mean, we hardly think of what we are about to receive. We're reduced to a state of quivering paranoia about whether we've been generous enough in our generosity.

And yet, why shouldn't we get what we want? Why is it, when I wanted a Journey Into Space Phase-Locked Neutron Blaster Module with real sparks and a siren loud enough to wake the victims it had just annihilated, I got a doll that wets its nappy?

That was last year. This year, I desperately wanted diving equipment. In October, I finally had to abandon my famous pre-metric 34-pint cylinder, the Black Pig. "It's failed the visual test, mate," they explained down at the Waterfront Warehouse.

I was mortified. "Are you absolutely sure?"

"Here, see for yourself. Just look through the hole in the side."

My old demand valve, a 1957 Hotpoint Lumpsucker IV, hasn't been the same since I replaced the diaphragm with the girlfriend's cap. It once froze up in the Caribbean; and besides, it's dreadfully heavy. Last year, it incurred an excess baggage charge on the Swansea-Cork ferry. It's also the reason I have front teeth like Freddie Mercury.

My drysuit, on the other hand, is anything but heavy. It would be best described as holes tied together with rubber bands. Only last week, the government of Zambongalesiland offered me 40 million b'nanos for it. They were proposing to stretch it between the banks of the M'banga River during the dry season to increase the rate of flow. Sadly, 40 million b'nanos are worth only 48p and in any case are non-negotiable outside Zambongalesiland.

Nevertheless, at my request, the Zambongalesi Trade Commission sent me a list of things costing 40 million b'nanos or less. This is it:

- A five-bedroom colonial-style residence in secure compound, with en suite diamond mine, stabling for ten gnus and a 20-acre yam plantation;
- 38 teenage slave girls (equivalent – two slave boys);
- 17 incorruptible members of the Zambongalesiland People's House of Representatives;
- 2lb sugar;
- 3.67 seconds at the Zambonga Hilton;
- No penicillin at all.

On the basis of some highly confidential information furnished by a friend in the commodities market, I accepted the offer and immediately invested the proceeds in two pounds of sugar.

Sure enough, next day, the Zambongalesi sugar crop failed, destroyed instantly by a rare bacterial infection called Monck's Conphorginsular Discafinating Moribundal Preconfascilitis (PNFT) – the only known cure for which is penicillin.

The effect on the price of sugar was entirely predictable. It soared from 40 million b'nanos to 180 million b'nanos in just under half an hour.

By Zambongalesiland standards, I was fantastically wealthy. I could now afford a 60-room neo-classical mansion on the shores of Lake B'ong, set in 400 acres of immensely fertile, gold-yielding savannah. I could, should I so wish, fill it with dozens of swooningly beautiful girls garnered from the bazaars and slave markets of all Africa (equivalent – four slave boys).

With a little tough negotiation, I could unwind amid the affluent splendour of the Hilton for almost ten minutes. I could effectively own the entire government of the country.

The penicillin would still present a bit of a problem, though.

My solution had the simplicity of real genius. Old drysuits had provided the key to my success. Therefore, I would reinvest my gains in more of the same.

Back in Sturminster Parva, I bought up 23 rotten, inadequately patched and malodorous suits, at least one of which had seen service in the Napoleonic wars.

Within days, I was back in drought-bound Zambongalesiland, preparing to embark upon a great safari, taking in all the major rivers and irrigation systems.

My scheme proved enormously successful. Too successful. When stretched across a water course, the suits actually allowed through twice the normal quantity of water. The country was devastated by catastrophic floods which swept away the Hilton and the Zambongalesi People's House Of Representatives, drowned 3698 slave girls (equivalent – five slave boys) and flattened several large, neo-classical mansions.

The only dubious up-side to the whole affair was that when the flood waters entered a bakery in N'gaga, they were soaked up by a hundred tons of bread. The mould which subsequently grew upon the bread turned out to be penicillin. At last, the country had an antidote to the scourge of Monck's Conphorginsular Discafinating Moribundal Preconfascilitis (HPBC).

However, this bacteriological breakthrough was of a purely academic significance, since the floods had also wiped out the entire sugar crop. But I digress.

Thanks to my dalliance in the international commodities market, I was now entirely drysuitless. I certainly couldn't afford a new one. Christmas was my only hope.

I took to leaving obvious clues about the house: bottles of dry white wine on the mantlepiece, juxtaposed with all the spades from my treasured 1978 Penthouse Pets canasta set.

I left the girlfriend's Next catalogue on her pillow, open at the men's tailoring section – along with a rich tea biscuit and a photostat of August's weather map for the Western Sahara.

I really thought I'd pulled it off when she smiled at me and said, "You can stop now. I get the hint."

Imagine my mounting excitement as Christmas Day approached. Each morning, I would analyse the size, shape and weight of the parcels under the tree, desperately searching for anything resembling the DUI crushed neoprene drysuit I knew was mine.

Imagine, then, my excruciating disappointment when I tore open my present to reveal the Journey Into Space Phase-Locked Neutron Blaster Module.

TRAVEL TIMES

Pages from the logbook
of a globe-trotting diver

"A *travel* tour de force. *From the outfall of the urea plant at Billingham to the outfall of the sewage treatment plant at Redcar, Blackford has been there, done that.*"

Outfall Monthly

Getting away from it all

THIS YEAR, the range of holidays on offer to divers is greater than ever.

At the inexpensive end of the market, you can enjoy three days on the *Silly Sod*, a converted pedalo working out of Greenford on the Grand Union Canal. The total cost of the holiday is £85 for divers, £50 for non-divers, and £7.50 for pedallers.

Norman 'Probably' Carlsberg, skipper of the *Silly Sod*, explains: "The big attraction of this holiday is definitely the fish. We've seen him twice already this year."

At the other end of the scale, a month's liveaboard on the late Robert Maxwell's yacht in the Indian Ocean with Tiara Tours of Lichtenstein is so expensive that it has to be booked a generation in advance. You simply take an endowment policy with a 50-year term and bequeath it to your natural child or nominated beneficiary in the event of your death.

Remember, however, that the value of your investments can go down as well as up. My own dear father signed up with Tiara back in the thirties and, thanks to the stock market crash of 1989, all I got was three days as a pedaller on the *Silly Sod*.

As diving has become more comfortable and accessible, so the nature of the diving holiday has changed. Where once we were perfectly happy to shave in the horse trough by the tent in the rain at Seahouses, we now demand something a little more sophisticated.

Indeed, the dedicated diving holiday is itself rapidly becoming a thing of the past, replaced by "double-interest" packages. This new sophistication has even permeated my own branch, where Nigel Fishwick is organising a two-centre Diving & Creative

Fretwork holiday this summer, in the Yucatan Peninsula and Birkenhead.

It's a bold and imaginative concept, but as I've already explained to Nigel, one that is almost certainly doomed to failure. The diving part of the holiday is in Birkenhead, for one thing, and Mexican fretwork is among the worst in the world.

Personally, I shall probably go to Papua New Guinea in August. It's a fascinating part of the world, largely undived. You sleep in longhouses in the rainforest with the natives, who live as they have done since the Stone Age. The price is £2000 per head, but they'll throw in a second head for £500.

Of course, as a famous journalist with DIVER, I get to dive all over the world. Why, last year I hardly had time to sit down. I'd no sooner unpacked after my January jaunt to Fishguard than I was off to Blear Rigg Pit, a flooded fertiliser mine near Middlesbrough, to cover the annual general meeting of the British Cryogenics Society. Sadly the meeting never really got under way, as all attempts to revive the chairman proved unsuccessful.

Then it was off to Suffolk, on the British Nuclear Fuels educational tour of Sizewell – a fascinating glimpse of the shape of things to come. The shape of the crustaceans was particularly fascinating; the advent of the three-clawed lobster has exciting implications for the catering industry.

I must say, writing for DIVER may not make you rich, but it certainly has its little perks. Since the Sizewell dive, my flat has been bathed in a green, iridescent glow – very restful on the eyes, and it does away entirely with the need for electric lights.

A sad development, to my mind, is the move towards individual holidays and away from the good, old-fashioned branch holiday. I'll always remember with affection the two weeks we spent on the picturesque Hebridean islet of Ailsa Craig (which in Gaelic means "God-forsaken little rock with bugger-all to recommend it").

The accommodation was spartan, but perfectly adequate for our needs. Colin and I slept between midnight and two, then Bomber and Norman took over the bed until four, and so on until we'd all 12 of us had a proper rest.

Food was plentiful – and although there is a limited number of ways in which to present heather and seagulls' eggs, things looked up considerably in Week Two when the locals sold us the matches; the best £10 I've ever spent.

I have to say, the natives were a funny lot. All three of them were odd to the point of eccentricity. They lived together in a turf hut with a sheep they called Grandad, and they drank a strange, blue spirit which they distilled in the rusty radiator of an abandoned De Dion.

I had assumed they were Hebrideans, born and bred, but it turns out they'd all been members of Woking Branch of the BSAC and had come to the island the previous summer on a Club expedition.

Considering the fact that their subscriptions had barely expired, they were hardly hospitable. When the bull ate Bomber's bivouac during the blizzard and we asked the one called Gordon if we could borrow his woolly hat, he simply replied, "Aw yer gred wussock, geet thurn wi' yer gorm faggot an' be doon!"

Not, I would venture, a remark designed to foster the atmosphere of understanding and camaraderie you might expect between members of an internationally respected sporting organisation.

A far cry, too, from the extraordinary quality of service now enjoyed by the diver in exotic foreign locations. Take the Virgin Islands, for instance, where I was lucky enough to dive recently.

There, merely to glance at your bottle is considered a mortal insult to the skipper. Your gear is swung aboard in a sling of female mink (so much softer than the pelt of the male), and so relaxing are the ministrations of the aromatherapist that you're hardly aware of the silk Pierre Cardin stab jacket as the dusky hostesses drape it lightly around your shoulders.

As I moved towards the rail, I was gently restrained by a graceful and manicured hand. "Why, Mistuh Blackford, sir," purred its owner, "don' you go exertin' your good self! You're on yo' vacation!

"Jes' you make yo' self comfortable and McKinley here'll go do yo' divin' for you. That's what he's paid fer, after all!"

To Siberia
with Marjory

AND ANOTHER thing. How is it that everybody gets the same baggage allowance, when some people are so much heavier than others? It's a travesty.

Take Marjory Rafferty-Ping Ho, for instance, the daughter of an Irish demolition contractor and a 250lb Cambodian horse masseuse.

Interestingly, the Ping Hos were the Irish side of the family, descendants, they claim, of the marauding warrior kings of Kazakstan who landed near Cork and founded the famous Irish dynasties of Ho Reilly, Ho Malley and Ho Neill.

As for the ancient Rafferty clan of Cambodia, space does not permit a full account of Padric Rafferty's 12,000-mile coracle odyssey from Dublin to Phong Peng, to spread the Christian gospel in Fishguard. Suffice it to say that his sense of timing matched his grasp of geography – he died a disappointed man in 12BC.

When describing Marjory, the words 'slight' and 'petite' do not spring unbidden to the tongue. 'Elfin' and 'svelte' are terms over which one would heedlessly skip as one scanned one's thesaurus for an appropriate epithet to express the essential quality of Marjory.

Not to put too fine a point on it, she once had a summer job with Cumbria Education Authority, demonstrating Archimedes' Principle to school children by stepping in and out of Lake Windermere.

At the Branch, they call her Larjory – but only very quietly, when she isn't there. For Marjory is endowed with huge physical strength.

When the van broke down near Exeter, it was Marjory who towed it to Plymouth. It was Marjory who won the Evinrude Three

Peaks Challenge, storming up Striding Edge with a 70hp boat engine under each arm. Marjory who beat the club compressor at blow football.

I suppose it was fate that drove us together. The Branch held a raffle to raise funds for essential alterations to the clubhouse. We'd had to apply for planning permission when Marjory joined, and the surveyors had insisted on extensive structural work.

Reinforcing the foundations proved to be a massive undertaking. But we managed to salvage the bow section of the *Torrey Canyon* which, along with a pair of 20m basalt megaliths from Avebury Rings, more or less did the trick.

Marjory and I were joint winners of the raffle, so we agreed to share first prize – a diving trip to the closed city of Bonk in northern Siberia.

Our Treasurer fixed it up. "We got an amazing deal," he enthused. "Apparently, they've only just opened up the place to tourists – you know, after the dioxin plant blew up and started the meltdown at the nuclear power station that sparked off the fire storm in the uranium mine and activated all the warheads in the submarine missile silos.

"You'll be the first Westerners ever to dive in the lake. It's a great honour."

"What's the diving like?" I enquired.

"Fascinating, I'm told. The local wildlife has adapted wonderfully well to the conditions. Look out for the giant amphibious white mice. There's a whole colony of them, near the crater where the genetic research laboratory used to be."

I noticed we didn't have return tickets. "No problem," beamed our Treasurer. "You get them when you leave. It's just the way they do things over there. When in Bonk, et cetera!"

As I always say, never look a gift horse, et cetera, so Marjory and I began our preparations.

It quickly became clear that baggage space was going to be a real problem. Marjory's drysuit alone accounted for two large dive bags. She'd fashioned it herself from the tarpaulin they used to shroud the hulk of the *Mary Rose* while they sprayed her with preserving fluid.

Her stab jacket incorporated no less than three of the lifting bags used in the filming of *Raise The Titanic*.

Then there were all the other items, essential to the success of a week's diving holiday – the teasmade, the waterbed, the pro croquet set, the lifesize portrait of Bonjour Pierre, winner of the 1926 Cheltenham Gold Cup, the power strimmer, Marjory's world-renowned collection of parking tickets, the stuffed remains of her grandmother's favourite coypu Maurice, all fifteen volumes of E.L. Norbert's *20 Years Among the Baktaars of Rumpistan* and a hoe.

Clearly, this strange compendium of impedimenta could not be contained in a conventional suitcase or even a trunk. Happily, Marjory had attended an auction of personal effects of the Russian royal family and had acquired, for the sum of $2.50, the Imperial kitchen sink from the winter palace at St Eriksburg, into which all her diverse possessions could be stowed with ease.

On the morning of our departure I arrived at Marjory's house at 6am. We just had time for a cuppa before the forklift showed up – then we were off.

There was the usual carry-on at the airport. I don't know – the whole business of international travel seems to become more fraught every year. For a start, the Siberoflot check-in was a Portakabin, 2 miles from the terminal in the quarantine area. One would-be passenger to Omsk had spent the last six months there in a wire mesh enclosure, existing on a diet of bonemeal biscuits and suffering the indignity of daily vet inspections.

Fortunately, they mistook Marjory for a famous Russian fashion model and we were treated like VIPs. Hardly any pistol whipping at all. Her luggage, however, was a different matter. Some hasty calculations on the back of an old military secret revealed that Marjory's stuff weighed slightly more than the aircraft. But somewhat less than Marjory herself.

It was I who came up with a solution. We would leave behind M's weightbelt (which was made up of worn helicopter parts strung on steel hawser), the euphonium and seven volumes of Norbert. The rest we would stack next to me on the aisle seat and Marj would travel as livestock in the cargo hold.

Once I'd made sure she'd been given food, water and fresh bedding, I sauntered along to the Siberoflot lounge for a samovar of iced cabbage sherry, the national tipple.

This, I reflected with satisfaction, was going to be the holiday of a lifetime.

* * * * * * * * *

THE TAXI DRIVER delivered a well-aimed blow to the hind-
quarters of his leading yak and we lurched out of the airport
towards town. It was none too soon for me. It was now 12 hours
since we had touched down, and I was exhausted by our long
interview with the immigration authorities. They had been under
the misapprehension that Marjory was an emergency food
shipment from Germany, and they were all set to distribute her
among the city's homeless. As mistakes go, I suppose it was an
understandable one.

In the end, we compromised. I managed to get her imported as
a crane. But we weren't out of the woods yet – they let her go only
on the condition that she started work next day on the foundations
of the new Margaret Thatcher Institute of Karaoke in Blink. But
we'd cross that bridge when we came to it. As we passed the city
limit, I was able to translate for Marjory the rather perfunctory
sign: *Welcome to Bonk, Twinned with Hiroshima. Population:* ~~395000~~
~~4700~~ *158.*

Another read: *Bonk Welcomes Trained Medical Personnel.* I
couldn't imagine why. Eventually, the cab pulled up outside our
hotel on Benny Hill Square and I paid off the driver with a Michael
Jackson single.

I must say, these Russians are sticklers for hygiene. We were
frisked at the door by a team of security men with geigercounters.

We checked in and went to our respective rooms. Marjory was
ushered to the Kalashnikov Suite, which had served as Bonk's
football stadium during the Stalinist era. It was in that very
apartment, I recalled, that Bonk Dynamo scored their legendary 7-0
victory over Accrington Stanley in the Omsk Sunday League semi-
final of 1936.

I had a smaller room, supposedly overlooking the lake –
which, to my surprise, seemed to have gone. Where should have
danced the glittering wavelets of Eastern Europe's biggest expanse
of fresh water, there was a desert of brown filth, broken only by
frozen explosions of orange and purple slime and the twisted
skeletons of domestic pets.

I felt a sudden twinge of home-sickness – it reminded me

irresistibly of the Arndale Centre in Middlesbrough.

When I pointed out to the porter that the view could not be said to live up to the description in the holiday brochure, he appeared discomfited. "Look! See!" I gesticulated expressively. "No lake, jah? Kaput!"

"Ah! Ze lake! Nyet! You are wrong. Zat iz ze lake!" And he added, by way of explanation, "It is always zis thick in July. You wanna thin lake, you go to Stoney Cove, isn't it."

It was not without some misgivings that I unpacked my gear in preparation for the next day's diving.

WE MET our dive guide outside the hotel at 09.00. His name was Azzsher. For the first three days of the holiday, I thought he had hay fever. He spoke no English and no Russian. Nor any French, Spanish or German. Nor Italian, Dutch or Swedish.

It turns out he spoke only Unculese, a pseudo-language, devised by his Uncle Vladimir, and wholly devoid of meaning. Claiming it was English, Vladimir had taught it to the nomadic tribesmen of Kazakstan – who had no reason to doubt him, of course, since they, too, knew no English. In this way he accumulated the air fare to London, where he planned to learn real English. When he arrived at Heathrow, he knew only two words – 'reading' and 'writing'. He spotted the former on the front of a waiting bus, and boarded it, imagining it would whisk him away to some institute of higher learning. Instead, it took him to that unexceptional town in Berkshire, where he worked for eight years as a bus conductor until he had saved enough to pay his fare back to Bonk. Interestingly, Unculese is still spoken in remote parts of Kazakstan – although, of course, nobody can understand it, including those who speak it.

But that's another story.

Azzsher watched us kit up on the prom, then led us into the lake. Or rather on to it. It was an odd sensation, walking on water. Our Diving Officer would have taken to it instantly.

I couldn't see for the life of me how we were to penetrate the amalgam of congealed effluent and raw sewage that covered the lake like the crust of some diabolical, poisonous pie.

But Azzsher had clearly done this before. He produced a sardine from behind his ear and tossed it on to the filth before him.

After a matter of seconds, we heard the shriek of a seagull and a large skua came barrelling down from a great height. I shall not forget the sound its beak made as it pierced the toxic scum – the sort of noise a rusty pitchfork makes when it ruptures the colon of a flatulent pig.

With a terrific splintering and groaning, the crust shattered. And Marjory disappeared into the murky soup below. I stared down into the blackness for a moment, then launched myself after her.

The swirling water (I use the term loosely) engulfed me and I plummeted down and down for what seemed an eternity. I hit bottom and glanced at my computer. It recorded a depth of 3m. There was no sign of Marjory. The water emanated a greenish phosphorescence and I could just make out the forms of strange, mutant submarine creatures. Several of the fish had developed satellite dishes, I noticed, and a small colony of sponges were playing backgammon for winkles.

It was then that the algae began to digest my drysuit, and my DV turned into putty between my teeth. Regretfully, I abandoned Marjory and struck out for the surface...

TRAVEL UPDATE: Marjory was eventually located by sonar and now forms the basis of an artificial reef. Blackford returned to England where he works part-time as a fuel rod at Sizewell B. Diving packages to Bonk are available through the Siberian tourist organisation, Brownpeace.

Have 'lung will travel

HAVE 'LUNG will travel. That's me – light-travelling free spirit of the diving world.

The cab company used to ask, "Heathrow or Gatwick?" Now it's just, "First or Concorde?"

My passport is so current, you get a shock from it. My tan is so deep, my bones don't show up on X-rays.

For travel, my friends, is an art. And like any art, it may be perfected only through practice.

Take my trip to Indonesia, for instance.

The call came as I was idling away an afternoon at DIVER, melting down our publisher's jitterbugging trophies for weightbelts.

The phone rang. Eventually, I raised a languid hand to the receiver. The Voice belonged to a beautiful woman. You could just tell. It was the sort of Voice they play to bees to boost honey production. If this Voice were to tell you your house had burned down, your car had been stolen and your wife had run off with the gypsies, you'd thank it from the bottom of your heart.

"How do you fancy," purred the Voice, "two or three weeks diving around the little-known, exotic, barely explored Togian Islands, perfectly proportioned beads of emerald set in white gold against a field of pure blue azure?"

To the ordinary man... tempting. But let's not forget who we're dealing with here. This is Andy Blackford, who is to diving as Terry Waite is to solitary confinement. Cosmopolitan, world citizen, multi-linguist and consummate aquanaut. In short, not easily impressed.

My reply was a model of professional reserve – cool and

guarded: "Oh, thankyouthankyouTHANKYOU! God, I'm so *honoured*! What can I possibly say, except, well, if there's anything – *anything* – I can ever do for you, just consider it done. You've simply no idea what this means to me as a writer and an artist. To know that someone appreciates at least a particle of what one strives and suffers to achieve is, well, simply *overwhelming*. I am yours. There. I've said it. Enough. So… yes! Yes, yes, YES, **YES!**"

It only remained to drop in on the GP for a couple of booster shots, toss a few things in a bag, and I was away.

As usual, Sam, my doctor, was the essence of brisk efficiency. He peered gloomily from his Mayfair apartment into the street below. "Y'know, Mercs aren't what they used to be. Time was when I could wait two years before trading up to a new one. I've only had the 300CE for a year and already there's a champagne stain on the rear arm rest. It'll have to go. But that's the tragedy of the modern world, isn't it, Andrew. Falling standards. And nobody *cares*. Not *really*.

"Still, that's enough about my problems. You're going… abroad. Right. In that case, you need… let's just see, now… ah, yes … polio, cholera, diphtheria, hepatitis, lassa, green monkey, bubonic, bulimia, ringworm, halitosis, shingles and indonesia. Sorry, that's where you're going, isn't it. Forget that, then. Any more countries in there? How about Diphtheria? No? Sure? Fine. Bend over."

I've never been so ill in all my life.

If they'd had the wit to take me to the isolation hospital, they'd have been fighting over which ward to stick me in. Displaying the symptoms of the World Health Organisation's Top 20 Killer Tropical Diseases, I was an Admissions Officer's nightmare.

Houseman 1: "Look at the pustules. I'm telling you, he's mine."

Houseman 2: "Piffle. Just look at the stools. Mauve. He's clearly one of ours."

Houseman 3: "Never mind the stools. Observe the tongue. Thick, leathery texture with horny mushroom-like protruberances – colour of rotting taramasalata on flock wallpaper. He's mine."

Houseman 4: "Hang on, hang on! Bollocks! Look at the glutinous, evil-smelling discharge from the eyeballs and the underarm glands. Note the foul excrescence from the ears, the hair loss, the gross swellings of the ankles and nipples. You'd have to be an idiot or a charlatan not to concede that he's mine."

As it turns out, nobody sent me anywhere, and I was far too ill to go under my own steam. So I lay there, oozing and pustulating, for a week – half medical textbook, half special effect from *Night of The Living Dead.*

When I recovered consciousness, I had 45 minutes to catch the plane. I grabbed my bag. Fortunately, my needs are few. I grabbed a couple of suits – old rags, really, that I picked up months ago at the Giorgio Armani show in Milan – a handful of silk shirts by Cuthbert of Jermyn Street, and five or six pairs of frogskin Gucci loafers.

Next, diving kit. I stuffed my IBM computer, keyboard, colour monitor and laser printer into my holdall. (My dive computer is designed to interface with a PC, and, after some experimentation, I've found it's better to dive with the PC and then download all the data on to the Suunto when you get home.)

I'd read somewhere that while the water is generally warm in Indonesia, the seas are characterised by dramatic thermoclines. Temperatures can vary by 10 degrees in the space of a metre. So I hacked my neoprene drysuit in half with a Stanley knife and bundled the bottom half into my dive bag along with a string vest.

Then there was the question of air. I wasn't at all sure there'd be any available on the Togian Islands. I mean, I've been stuck for a fill in Swanage before now – let alone on some remote atoll in the precise epicentre of nowhere. Should I take enough bottles for a fortnight's diving? In the end, common sense prevailed. I settled for a compressor instead.

I'd just finished packing my bible and the complete works of Shakespeare, and was in the middle of choosing my eight favourite gramophone records when the phone rang. It was the Voice.

"Sorry," it simpered, "Norway has invaded the Togian Islands, the boat has been hijacked by Cambodian pirates and the airline has gone into receivership. The trip's off."

It took me only a moment to regain my composure. "That's OK," I replied airily. "I was rather busy anyway."

Taking the rough
– or the smooth

WHAT'S the difference between a Diving Holiday and a Diving Expedition?

I've just come back from a Diving Expedition, so nobody is better qualified to explain the difference than I am.

The most important difference is the plumbing. On a DH (Diving Holiday) you can expect a certain minimum standard of sophistication and hygiene in the sanitary arrangements.

On a DE (Diving Expedition) the toilets are connected directly to Hell. Instead of the usual ceramic pedestal, that monument to Civilisation, there is merely a reeking hole, a tunnel to the (forgive me) bowels of the Earth, from which pump forth the foulest vapours of the underworld.

On a DH, the diving is predictable. You know what you're going to get. The sites are explored, established – the guides are walking encyclopedias of local knowledge.

On a DE, nobody knows anything about anything. Worse, the locals pretend to know everything. They sniff the wind, gaze intently at the horizon, shuffle about in little circles while shading their eyes with their hands – then tell you, with astonishing accuracy, precisely where the wreck isn't.

Often, on a DE, the sites have never been dived before. In my experience, there is usually a perfectly good reason for this. They're crap. It's the same reason there isn't a Club Med in the Gobi Desert, or a Hilton Hotel on Baffin Island.

We divers are constantly seduced by the lure of the unknown. We daydream of the untold wonders that await us beneath the billows. After all, we reason, two-thirds of the world's surface is covered by water.

But it never occurs to us to ask why.

If our planet were created by any kind of rational, superhuman intelligence, then surely it would have covered up the less successful bits?

I would. It's common sense. You've done the soaring, snowcapped Himalayas; you've bashed out the Amazon rain forests and the sexy one-offs like Monument Valley and the Grand Canyon. Even the Sahara has a certain barren majesty.

All the critics agree that the rest is pretty tedious by comparison. So what do you do? You open the sluices and drown it under five miles of water.

This achieves two objectives. First, in PR terms, it neatly plasters over the cracks in the Creation and enhances the public perception of the Supreme Being. Second, it invests the greater part of the Earth with a sense of mystery and romance, which generally makes life more fun for everybody.

It goes without saying that you'll encounter far more wildlife on an Expedition than on a Holiday.

On a DH, you might see a lionfish, a moray, a French angel or two, a turtle, a reef shark, a thousand varieties of coral.

On a DE, if my recent trip is anything to go by, you'll encounter mussels, more mussels, fleas, bed bugs, mites, mosquitoes, gnats, wasps, tsetse flies, hornets and half a million more biting, blood-sucking, stinging, vicious, poisonous little bastards, most of them invisible.

On a DH, people fall over you to make you comfortable: "Is your room to your liking, sir?"; "How did you find the thermidor, sir?"; "Did the Chablis match your expectations, sir? It *was* the '64 Grand Cru, sir."

A DE, on the other hand, isn't a DE unless you're surrounded either by surly, hatchet-faced natives who spit at your feet ("Whaddya want, Mister? Ah'm as a-busy as hell") or by brilliant, whinging beggars who contort their limbs into the most unimaginably grotesque parodies of human form. They plead for 5 centimos or bolivars or balthazars, and live just over the hill in service condos with sunken Jacuzzis in all five bathrooms.

On a Holiday, you get to use gleaming kit, bright, slick and silicon-greasy. On an Expedition you get (believe me) a Russian twinset in fall-out grey and rust, with a pillar valve compared to which Peter's finger in the dyke is state-of-the-art.

On an Expedition, your air is like the dying breath of a syphilitic wart-hog. It came from the onboard compressor which, in better days, pumped the methane from the septic tank of a Calcutta fever hospital.

On a DH, you can complain. "I'm sorry, but quite frankly the toast wasn't so much overdone as cremated, the bed felt like a giant condom stuffed with pigs' trotters, and the view reminded me of the last time I was sick in the toilet."

On a DE, you have no recourse. You are expected to eat the offal involuntarily regurgitated by the Evil Dead, to sleep with blindworms, to wash in re-cycled goat urine. And you're expected to love it.

And the amazing thing is, you do.

There is something about an Expedition that brings out the man in us – especially in the women.

A hundred years ago, half the world was pink. And if you think about it, apart from Surrey, the pink bits were the ones with leprosy, scrofula and beri beri, cholera and green monkey fever, typhus and typhoons.

They were the bits with noon temperatures of 45°C, seven-year droughts and annual rainfalls exceeding 300 inches; the bits with aboriginal inhabitants who ate you before they killed you, then wore your head on a belt about their purple-painted loins.

We didn't colonise Belgium, did we, or the nice bits of France? Too comfortable by half. Not nearly enough loathsome diseases or rabid animals.

Once we'd eradicated all the diseases and turned the cannibals into Methodists, the Empire was no fun any more, so we gave it back.

But this left us without a frontier. Without the potential for horrible discomfort, spine-snapping terror, incurable infection, we were denied the opportunity to be really British.

So what did we do? We founded the BSAC, and the rest, as they say, is history.

The Blackford clan head for the not-quite sizzling Skelligs

WHAT A SUMMER! Can you remember anything like it? Of course you can. There was 1976, for a start. I was working in Holland at the time and my office melted. The roof tar poured on to my desk and we were all evacuated. Except for my assistant, Wim, who was never found.

One day, in the far distant future, archaeologists from another star system will crack open a nodule of fossilised bitumen and there he'll be, perfectly preserved, grasping a cheese sandwich.

From this, they will deduce the existence of a 20th century food cult, the high priests of which were mummified with their favourite foodstuffs, so as not to go hungry in the afterlife.

Before that there was 1964, when I fell in love with Margery Chapman, who was blonde and worked in the Sandside Café, Runswick Bay. Just for the privilege of gazing cow-eyed at her completely unresponsive features, I was forced to buy 40 bottles of Coke a day. After a week, I was bankrupt and my teeth had developed the consistency of gruyère cheese. I didn't even get the money back on the bottles – I wanted her to think me debonair.

But this summer was special. It was the first really hot summer of my diving career.

Consequently, I went to Ireland, where it is never hot and where they stoically endure the permadrizzle – the soft flannel of precipitation that drifts in from the watery wastes of the Atlantic and flops damply on to the sodden peninsulas of the far West. Where we were.

It is one of the eternal mysteries of County Kerry that, while you could conduct a census of the population on the fingers of one hand, and while there are endless tracts of empty land – the result of the Famine, presumably, and the subsequent waves of emigration – the dwellings are generally the size of a garden shed.

Our cottage was no exception. In fact, it was the size of one of *their* garden sheds. Most of it was occupied by the water heater which, so rumour had it, was the converted reactor of a Russian nuclear submarine, wrecked on the treacherous Skellig Rocks. It could have heated the whole of Dublin effortlessly. It even heated the *cold* water.

Eamon, sheep farmer and electrician, came to fix it. Between long, anecdotal interludes and observations of a highly philosophical tenor, he clanked and puffed and chuckled and muttered mild blasphemies. When his red, round face emerged from the cupboard over the fireplace, it was obvious that technology had defeated him. "Sure that's a queer one, is that. I'm blowed if I can fully comprehend it. I tink… I only *tink*, mind … that it's the weather that'll be the cause of it. What with the sun beatin' down upon the roof, and causin' the excess of the heat."

Outside, the permadrizzle was drawing a misty veil over the mountains and drenching our dog. In these parts, the sun enjoys an almost legendary status – like Robin Hood does in England.

If the heater suffered from a surfeit of zeal, the 'welcoming warmth of an open fire' (sic: the travel brochure) was a martyr to the opposite affliction. It burned blocks of peat, which were almost like *objets d'art*. Or rather it didn't. It was like trying to burn cement. They glimmered momentarily with sad little sparks, then went out. After that, the peat seemed actually to radiate coldness. After a day or two, we gave up trying to light the blocks and took them home instead as *objets d'art*.

In retrospect, I think the Chilly Peat was a cunning device, designed to drive us into the Deaf Fiddler. This was the best of the four pubs in Creep, a tiny village where, statistically, the most popular profession is that of publican.

The pub quickly became our daughter's favourite place on Earth. In all her three months, she'd never seen the match of it. She could be wailing loud enough to shake down the walls of the Garden Shed – but take her to the Deaf Fiddler, stick her in a corner, and within seconds she'd be grinning like a lottery winner.

The diving was spectacular. Once you'd managed to sort out where the sky ended and the sea began, and you'd jumped in just exactly between them, you were in big ocean water. The clear grey light filtered down to 40m at least, playing upon flat diagonal slabs of granite the size of football pitches and gleaming with mats of jewel anemones.

On one occasion, we were tailed by a nosy seal, though we saw none on the surface. When we surfaced, however, our thunder was stolen by the non-divers on the boat, who had followed a 1m long leatherback turtle.

The most spectacular dive was on the Skelligs – the two absurdly island-like islands, 12 miles off the Kerry shore. One was occupied only by cormorants and puffins – you could smell it a mile off – the other was the site of an ancient monastery. The monks lived in queer, stone beehives at the very summit of this tree-less granite crag, eating gulls' eggs, in order to be closer to God.

We travelled out to it on a summer's day in a twin-engined hardboat. Despite this there was big-time queasiness all round. Rowing to the Skelligs in January in a cow-hide skiff doesn't even bear thinking about. Nor do the periodic visits to the monastery by the Vikings – flaying Christians alive was the Viking equivalent of bar billiards.

But the diving was huge. The massive Atlantic waters swayed and pulled, even at 20m, and boulders like houses (not sheds, note) were strewn chaotically about. Dead man's fingers and plumose anemones as thick as your arm; big, slow dogfish and wrasse the size of grouper – the wuthering deeps seemed to beckon you downwards, where dark and ancient mysteries awaited.

Thank heavens for the Dead Fiddler, which simultaneously beckoned you upwards to where dark and ancient Murphys awaited.

The ultimate in cordon-bleu diving

I'VE JUST returned from the Caribbean. There, I learned that one can only sex a parrot under general anaesthetic.

I'm sure the same would have been true of myself, after diving the Farnes last March.

The parrot in question was the mascot of the *Sea Cucumber* – a majestic schooner that might have drifted out of the Bermuda Triangle after a hundred years AWOL, but was, in fact, younger than the parrot.

The parrot was called Captain Loretto (although in the absence of any anaesthetic, it might easily have been Captain Loretta).

Captain L was 109. In the days before the wireless, he was trained to bear news of imminent bad weather from island to island. This explains the disproportionate number of Hurricane Pollys in the 1890s. During the frequent tropical storms that afflict the Windward Isles, he can still be heard to scream: "Forces of 8! Forces of 8!"

You may be wondering what the special significance of this parrot is. So, I confess, am I. I simply wasn't paying attention. I had intended to use the parrot Loretto as a neat, literary device, a mere introduction to the central theme of this story. And yet, half an hour later, I find I'm still rambling aimlessly on about the wretched bird, with nothing to show for it but two hundred words of unfocussed, mindless blather.

I can only apologise and move quickly on to the aforementioned 'central theme' of my piece: namely, how altogether superior an experience is Caribbean diving to the cheerless grind we are forced to endure here in our domestic waters.

As my age approaches that of Captain Loretto (that parrot

again) I find I appreciate those little luxuries available when each dive costs more than one's monthly mortgage repayment.

I know it shouldn't really take three Swedish men in starched white uniforms to pre-warm one's snorkel to sea temperature, but what the hell?

And I don't care who knows it: I was privately tickled to be lowered to the RIB in a mink sling. (If you saw my black leatherette thong, you'd understand why the mink tickled the privates.)

This was *cordon bleu* diving at its self-indulgent best. Even our air was special – collected in the stately homes of Europe's oldest and most noble families, then carefully compressed and decanted into our titanium bottles by the Carmelite nuns of St Vincent.

It was fascinating to think that the air one was breathing was last exhaled by a French *duc* or Prussian *junker* with a duelling scar. Apparently, until quite recently, one could request the air from the Marquis of Blandford's private apartments. But following several cases of nitrogen narcosis in only 5m of water, the option was reluctantly withdrawn.

And then, of course, there is the diving experience itself. What could match the vibrant kaleidoscope of colour, form and texture that is a Caribbean reef?

The *Sea Cucumber*'s diving team have perfected the ultimate diving experience. Over dinner, one is invited to choose from an extensive menu of marine life forms. You simply tick the boxes next to those plants and creatures you would prefer to see during the next morning's dive and the ship's marine biologists do the rest.

Strolling on the aft deck in the early hours of the morning, I could hear them working away tirelessly:

"Now, Cabin 108. Turtle (leatherback)…"

"Check."

"… spotted drum…"

"Drum."

"Shark…"

"Reef or lemon?"

"Er… hasn't specified."

"Reef then. Next?"

"Smooth trunkfish or similar."

"Can do you a honeycomb?"

"Excellent. How are we for snowflake morays?"

"Low. Green any good?"

And so on. The system worked perfectly. Just to test them, I asked to see a Jif bottle and the front page of the *Sport*. Sure enough, next day, there they were. For all the world, it could have been Kimmeridge Marine Conservation area.

The only thing that gave the game away was the stone fish. It was the same specimen in St Lucia and Grenada. It was unmistakable – perfectly camouflaged, completely invisible. I missed it both times. It didn't fool me for a moment. Oh, and in Grenada the Queen Angel winked at me. But otherwise, full marks.

Perhaps the most exciting experience of the trip was listening to the brain coral thinking. The first colony we came upon was very young. The dive guide attached the electrodes and switched on the audio encephalograph. All you could hear was a low gurgling sound, punctuated by moans of "F-o-o-o-d! F-o-o-o-d!"

The second head was altogether more mature:

"What are we here for?" it agonised. "Is there a God? And if there is, has he got antlers like the elkhorn says?"

Yet another chunk was of a poetic frame of mind:

"We are all of us in the gutter," it mused, "but some of us are looking at the starfish."

Upon surfacing, our tanks were removed by virgins and our solid gold weightbelts replaced in the RIB's safe.

Rockafeller and Vanderbilt, our boat handlers, broke out the 1898 Courvoisier Reserve, while our coxswain, Gloria Schiffer (Claudia's better-looking sister) smoked a Romeo y Julietta for me.

My wide-brimmed panama hat was chilling nicely in the boat's hat cooler. Anna and Myra, twin Russian concert pianists, were limbering up, prior to applying the Piz Buin to my pectorals.

All was entirely well with the world, I reflected. How different it all was from my last trip to Stoney Cove, when after two minutes in that lightless cocktail of crushed ice and waterborne infection, the circulation was only restored to my legs by a severe drubbing from a dwarf with a dead rat.

How very fortunate I was, nay privileged, to experience such glamour and sumptuous luxury, without having to practise as a dental surgeon in Cleveland, Ohio, like everyone else on board.

Thank you Mister Eaton. Thank you DIVER.

A good Oman

IN THE GULF, winter only works part-time. It clocks on in late afternoon, and works through till 9am when summer takes over for the day shift.

But now it was five o'clock and already the sun was crashing in flames behind a rip-saw of black basalt crags. At the foot of the mountains, the fantastic, golden dome of the Al Bustan Palace hotel flung the last rays away across the bay.

Behind us, the highway swooped down to touch the shore, then curved away up into the desert again, like the trail of a banking jet, frozen in concrete.

"Twenty years ago," offered Sunil, our guide, "there were just seven kilometres of paved road in Oman."

"How many are there today?" I enquired.

"Nine," replied Sunil. Then he laughed manically, his teeth gleaming in the dusk. "Only joking, only joking!"

In fact the development of Oman, a country bigger than the British Isles, is one of the unsung wonders of the modern world.

Until 1974 the country was a fiefdom, ruled over by a dynasty of Sultans who had done nothing to halt the country's decline from commercial supremacy. (Remember the heady days when Oman cornered the frankincense market? No? OK.)

The son of the last Sultan, though, was a restless, intelligent type who didn't see why Oman should be condemned to the perpetual twilight of the Middle Ages when her neighbours – Qatar, Bahrain, Abu Dhabi – were enjoying all the benefits of Western technology, thanks to their vast oil revenues.

And here's a lesson for Sultans everywhere: if you're going to send your bolshy kid into exile, don't send him to Sandhurst.

The lad came home to Oman with a formidable grasp of military tactics. There followed a bloodless coup, it was dad's turn for the extended holiday in London, and Oman was on course, full speed ahead for the twentieth century.

First to go was history. Down came the ancient palace of his forefathers – up went the astonishing new one, all white, green, gold and bulbous, as if the set designer from Thunderbirds had stolen a billion dollars, taken acid and built a monument to Ali Baba in the style of the Odeon, Ongar.

Next came the roads, curving gracefully through the barren landscape, lined with hundreds of thousands of palms, each one watered daily according to the dictates of the Sultan's beautification programme.

(The Arab culture has no tradition of representational art. Not that this has deterred the Sultan in his ambition to make Oman look like a proper western country: don't be dismayed if you come across a 7m high statue of a coffee pot on the central reservation – or a fibreglass elk perched on some rocky protruberance in the exact epicentre of absolutely nowhere.)

Schools followed fast – free, compulsory education in Arabic – then hospitals and clinics. And if they can't mend you in Oman, they'll ship you off to a man who can, in England or Canada or America.

Foreign managers and workers poured in at the invitation of the government: Pakistanis and Indians, mostly, and Sri Lankans like our Sunil. But every foreign manager has to train up the Omani who will succeed him. That must be tough – rather like sawing off the branch you're sitting on.

Among the expatriate workers, of course, are the British military and their support workers. And it is this plucky bunch who were largely responsible for exploring the diving potential of Oman.

The coastline stretches for a thousand miles, and apart from a few miles to the north and south of Muscat and Salalah, it's more or less virginal.

Out there in the great void, concrete motorways soon crumble into rutted tracks. The temperature soars to Regulo 8 and there's no fresh water. So for divers, the solution would seem to be a liveaboard. Hah! There aren't any. The Holiday Inn at Salalah has

its own dhow, but that's little more than an exotic hardboat.

Basically, the diving is like the Red Sea; only rather more oceanic in character and with plankton blooms that can interfere with photography.

In a week, we barely scratched the surface. There were some stand-out moments. Like when we eased our big speedboat through a rocky inlet south of Muscat into a shallow lagoon, surrounded by fawn and biblical hills. We were watching an eagle balancing on fierce, hot poles of air, when the mirror of the sea was smashed by the joyous arc of a bottle-nosed dolphin – and then a pod of fifteen, maybe more, with their young. I grabbed a mask and tumbled over the side to watch them streaking along the sandy bottom, ten metres or so down.

We flew the 900 miles down from Muscat, the northern capital, to Salalah on the Yemen border. During the flight we saw…

nothing. Just the endless wilderness: the sun-baked rock, rucked and scored into whorls, ridges and wadis, the doodlings of a bored god.

If the Martians mounted a reconnaissance mission to central Oman, they'd fax back: "Zilch. Doodly squat. Planet lifeless. Suggest we try Venus. Out."

And yet, when you view Oman in the context of the whole Arabian peninsula, it looks positively crowded – a densely populated coastal strip before you get into the real, serious emptiness of Saudi Arabia.

As you approach Salalah, you see an extraordinary thing: a cloud. Then another, and another. And looking down, you begin to make out patches of olive drab among the rock and sand. Then a tree and a field, and soon the land is carpeted in green, and the sky towers with castles of cumulus.

The reason: Salalah catches the Indian monsoon. Every year, during the summer months, it drowns in tropical rain. The temperature plummets from 50 degrees to an almost-bearable 35, and the coastal plain bursts with corn and sugar cane, mango and banana. The sheer walls of the high sierra are swathed in fog – and the mountain roads are strewn with the corpses of camels, mown down by madmen in landcruisers.

The problem became so acute that the government built new villages on the lowlands – summer homes for the nomadic hill people, away from the fog and the 4x4 camel killers.

They've made it unprofitable to sink a "ship of the desert", too: the offence carries a statutory fine of $6000.

MY DIVING was out of the Holiday Inn, and was provided by the southern off-shoot of the biggest outfit in Muscat, Sunny Days Diving. Most of the exploration so far has been undertaken on a hit-and-miss basis by members of a BSAC branch, situated at a nearby air base, so you still get the feeling that something momentous might lie just around the next boulder.

And it does: during our dhow trip, a glance at the chart suggested an interesting site under an overhanging promontory. Nobody, including the boys from the base who had joined us for the day, had ever dived the site. Within minutes, two of our party had stumbled on a cave full of sleeping sharks. (The divers reversed out of the cave, quietly humming lullabies in Arabic.)

When not aboard the dhow, you just bung your stuff in the back of a jeep and bump and grind away into the desert. Spot a likely little inlet, kit up and waddle in. There are no established sites, no buoys, no transits. You just trust to your intuition and make it up as you go along.

On one such dive, we crawled agonisingly over a shore of coral skewers and long-spined urchins, and found ourselves in a garden of table corals, each formation 10m across or more. Gigantic jewfish lurked between the plates, and snowflake morays, some of them 2 or 3 metres long, snaked sinuously around the stems.

There were no signs of human visitation whatsoever – no tell-tale broken sprigs of fire coral, no up-rooted gorgonia – just an immaculate oasis of peace and plenty, a haven for shoals of angel fish and broom-tailed wrasse, for breathtaking nudibranchs, for wide-eyed puffers, lion fish, guitar sharks – all in an area not much bigger than our training pool, back home in London.

That you can simply stagger into the water, more or less at random, and encounter such a profusion and diversity of life, is both exhilarating and frustrating. Exhilarating because you're almost guaranteed a captivating dive – frustrating because you know that the truly extraordinary might be just around the next corner. Or more likely, just a mile or so out to sea. Whale sharks, for instance, are reasonably common off the coast of Oman, as are oceanic bottle-nosed dolphins, manta rays and tuna.

Nevertheless, there is nothing to beat the feeling of anticipation you feel as you kit up in the heat and stillness of some remote lagoon, with no sign of human habitation for 50 miles in any direction, knowing that nobody else has ever seen what you are about to see.

Put aside the fascination of a new country, hurtling into the modern world with real energy and imagination, forget the beauty and drama of its landscape, the warmth and generosity of its people – what Oman really offers the diver is the chance to realise the ambition that made him want to dive: to explore, to discover and to be First.

Madeira (not the cake, not the wine: the place)

IT TOOK mankind a million years to discover Madeira, which is amazing, because on a clear day you can see it from Land's End.

It was Henry the Navigator who first noticed it. Not Henry the Eighth, nor Henry the Serial Killer nor, for that matter, Henry the Especially *Good* Navigator. Because, in reality, he only got as close as Porto Santo, the next island: smaller, flatter and altogether less interesting.

His log merely reports, "Oh, and by the way, noticed a bunch of cloud a way off. Might be land. Someone should check it out sometime. Or not. Hey! Who gives a? Ciao! Henry."

Poring over his log 400 years later, I decided there might just be something in it. I resolved to risk everything in an act of blind faith to follow in the wake of Henry – to go and check out that "bunch of cloud" for myself.

Weeks of meticulous research and exploration, endless nights of hope and despair, were eventually rewarded. There really was a Madeira. And Air 2000 flew there once a week.

It's hard to describe the feeling of triumph I experienced, knowing that I had achieved what Henry The Navigator had failed to. And yet it was an elation mixed with humility. For without Henry's early work, how could I have made that step into the unknown and booked those two economy returns from Gatwick to Funchal?

There are no giants. We stand upon the shoulders of those who go before us.

Funchal has the shortest runway in Europe. Once, at a party hosted by *The Guinness Book Of Records*, I met the World's Fastest-Decelerating Man: 120mph to nought in 6 inches. (He drove a

Formula One racing car into a stone wall.) As we touched down, I suddenly knew how he must have felt.

Next time, I travel by Harrier Jump Jet.

The town itself is fascinating Portuguese colonial – every elegant cornice, fountain and architrave, reflecting the fabulous, ill-gotten wealth of an empire's merchant princes.

Scorpio Divers, on the other hand, is situated in a kind of art deco lido after the *Titanic* school of architecture, all decks and railings and sweeping curves of concrete icing. We turned up four days after the worst storm the island had suffered in 50 years.

Great cataracts had thundered down from the mountains, killing two people and sweeping 30 brand new Mercedes from their showroom into the sea, which retaliated by bashing the living daylights out of the shoreline.

The storm had even buckled Scorpio's heavy steel storm shutters and shoved them through their windows as if they were rice paper.

All of this was, however, pretty hard to imagine as we kitted up in the sleepy morning sunshine for our first (shore) dive. The site known as the Island is a 50m stack of rock within easy finning distance of the Lido steps – a pleasant and undemanding debut, which under normal circumstances would have been dressed in a cloak of weeds and sponges, but which the storm had stripped bare.

Squat lobsters, urchins and pretty sub-tropical fish (including Madeira's "national fish", the scorpion) abounded.

Apart from a pretty little cave dive, the rest of our programme was boat-based. Loading yourself and your equipment from the sea wall on to an inflatable was a decidedly Atlantic experience, and more than once I had cause to admire the skill of our Swedish guide, Johannes, as he played the boat like a prize salmon on a pair of running lines.

The offshore sites were quite challenging. The Scorpio crew seemed surprised by the strength of the currents – perhaps they were the aftermath of the storm – and we had to abandon a couple of dives for more sheltered locations.

Once you were in, though, the experience was rewarding. If you know the Canaries, much of the flora and fauna will be familiar. Squid, octopus, arrow crabs, moray. But there is a distinctly oceanic undertone, too – a subdued energy in the water, a sense of scale.

The tide sucks and tugs on vicious pinnacles of igneous rock, tooth sharp, while barracuda glint and sway above like metal kestrels. In the crannies, parrot fish graze with triggers and damsels, while a flotilla of big amberjack cruises in from the vast ocean expanses beyond.

In one hole, you'll come across a pair of green morays – in the next, a big conger. Always this strange mixture of tropical and temperate, a submarine microcosm of the island itself, where banana plantations steam and swelter within spitting distance of moorland, moss and chilly pine forests.

Madeira is a triumph of optimism over geography. Imagine a vast, volcanic crater, 1500 feet deep and sliced in half vertically. At the narrow, bottom end is the harbour and the town of Funchal fans out, ever-upwards until the higher suburbs can be glimpsed only occasionally through the swirling cape of cloud that drapes the great peaks behind.

All the more baffling that the average age of visitors to the island (the British ones, at any rate) is 103. To venture more than 6m from their hotels they must have their Zimmer frames adapted so that the front legs are 15cm shorter than the rear.

Local historians recall the notorious Bath Chair Races of the 1890s when Madeira was terrorised by a gang of geriatric hooligans. Drunk to the point of insensibility upon the fortified wine for which the island is famous, they raced their invalid carriages down the vertiginous road from Monte to Funchal.

Some attained speeds in excess of 80 miles per hour and were quite unable to stop when they reached the seafront. One particularly reckless contestant careered through Reid's Hotel, hurtling past reception and disrupting a tea dance in the Palm Lounge before crashing through the French windows into the Atlantic, 20m below.

Her remains were never recovered. Most probably, she was consumed by the *espada,* a huge eel that lives exclusively below the 600m mark – so deep, in fact, that nobody has ever seen a live specimen. So great is the pressure change on the way up, that the fish are always DOA.

The Madeiran fishermen know exactly where to find the

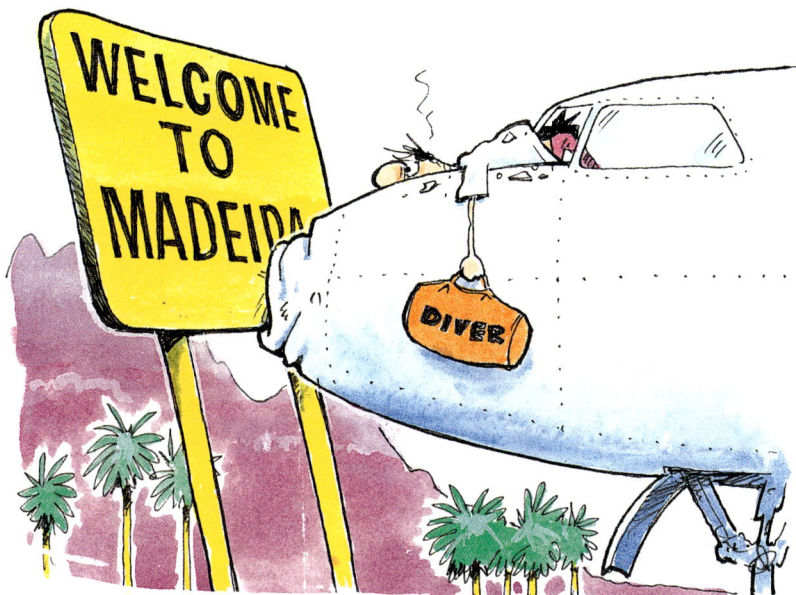

espada, but how they do it is a mystery. They use no modern navigational aids, steering entirely by the stars and the waves and the infallible instinct of centuries.

Well, not quite infallible.The proprietor of Scorpio Divers recounts the tale of a fisherman who radioed for assistance because he was lost. When asked for his position, he hadn't got a clue. He had no compass. He described the course he'd taken from Funchal in terms of currents and cloud patterns. Even with a full-scale air and sea search, it took two days to find him.

The Atlantic is very big. And Madeira is right in the middle of it, 500 miles from the African coast. The Canaries are a lot closer to the Dark Continent, and so enjoy what is basically a Saharan climate. Madeiran weather is more like, well, depending on whether you're standing over *here* or 2m away over *there,* Ecuador's, or South Carolina's. Or Manchester's.

For instance, it was cold and windy when we touched down at the Doll's Airport. But 5 miles and 76 heart-stopping hairpin bends away in Funchal, it was warm and sunny. Microclimates.

Head upwards and the differences become even more

dramatic. Being an idiot, I ran from the seafront to Monte which, for much of the day, is obscured by the cloud that hangs around the peaks. It was cool and damp up there, and I was impressed by the difference a half-hour's jog could make.

But when, later, we rented a car (Seat Marbella: no gears, no brakes, no tyres) and drove across the island, the climatic change was truly astonishing.

From Monte we wound interminably up through ancient pine forests, where the clouds got stuck in the trees and hung there in swathes, pierced by beams of watery sunlight.

Everywhere was excited water, dashing down ferny channels and hurtling over rocky cliffs in sparkling cascades. Jurassic Park meets the Scottish Highlands.

High, high up, on the very watershed of the island, we stopped for a drink in a log cabin straight out of the Canadian Rockies. A torrent of mad white water charged past the window as a barman in a roll-neck sweater served us mulled wine by an open fire.

An hour before and 1300m below, we'd been sunbathing on the poop deck of the *Titanic* after a dive amid sub-tropical fish in water so warm (21°C even in November) that a wetsuit was little more than a formality.

And therein is the real fascination of Madeira – its sheer, fantastic diversity. You can spend the morning in the rain forests, walking (or in my case, crawling) along the *levadas* – the precipitous and terrifying canals that deliver water from the high peaks to the banana fields of the south shore. A couple of hours later, you can be diving with Scorpio's Pedro, one of Portugal's finest underwater photographers, tickling groupers the size of St Bernard dogs.

There's really nowhere on earth quite like it.

MIXED TIMES

A broad view of divers and diving

"In diving, there are the Cans and the Can'ts. Andy Blackford, I'm afraid, has always been a complete Can't."

John Weinberg, PADI/BSAC Instructor

All aboard with the cheque-book boaters!

RIGHT. So you've scraped together the £250 for the wetsuit, £250 for the DV, £250 for the stab jacket, £250 for the cylinder, £250 for the vile pink and green fins, £250 for the new dive tables, £250 for the low-volume mask carved from the single block of crystalline Bolivian bauxite, and £2500 for the membership of your branch. With some justification, you imagine that you might be equipped to go diving.

Wrong. There's still the small matter of finding £25,000 for the boat.

The bloody boat.

Boats are the single most serious downside of diving in the UK. In British waters, you simply have to go by boat.

In the Red Sea, you kit up on the shore and saunter into the sea. The moment the water level is higher than you are, you're in a fantastic coral wonderland, teeming with marine life.

In the North Sea, you kit up in the car park, slither dangerously down the cliff path, stumble, swearing, over weed-slick rocks, trip on the rusty, jagged spout of the sewage outfall, and crash into the grey-brown consommé that passes for the sea.

Then you flounder blindly about for 20 minutes like a blenny with a ruptured swim bladder, searching vainly for periwinkles on the rotting stalks of the impenetrable kelp forest until you crawl thankfully on to the shore again, like one of our carboniferous ancestors emerging from the primeval slime, festooned with the latex consequences of AIDS education.

Not that your English Channel's any better. I remember diving from Brighton beach, once, with the branch. In stark contrast to our expectations of silver tableware, Victorian timepieces, rare coins, signet rings and jewel-encrusted bangles, all we had to show for three hours of sub-zero temperatures and nil visibility was an alloy spoon, a dead cocker spaniel, and the broken nose sustained by the Training Officer when he swam smack into a pier support.

Like it or not, you've got to have a boat. And the people who make boats cottoned on to this about 15 years ago. Until then, you could pick up a Zodiac inflatable for a couple of hundred quid. It was a never-ending source of fun, watching the novice trying to get the stringers in with the tubes inflated.

Even today, it never fails to raise a smile when someone recalls how Nigel Fishwick got his private parts caught between the boat boards that Easter in the snow off Drake's Island.

Personally, I'll never forget the time Norman Melsom punctured the Humber with his stiletto heels, 12 miles off Beachy Head. How we laughed – especially when it turned out there wasn't room in the chopper for Norman. We left him trying to paddle the flaccid husk of the inflatable back to shore with a fin lashed to a whip aerial. When he finally hove into sight at dawn the next day, he looked like a drunken fly on a fried egg.

I remember, too, my boat handling course in Norfolk. When Deric Ellerby complained that he had trouble getting his boat on the plane, I said I wasn't surprised and wouldn't it have been cheaper to leave the boat at home and hire another for the duration of the holiday?

Those were the days.

Then the boat industry got wise. Divers, they reasoned, were fanatical idiots with more money than sense. Therefore, they concluded, if they were to charge for an outsized kiddies' dinghy the price of a country cottage with three acres in Dorset, divers would whinge for 10 minutes, then cough up.

The same divers, incidentally, who suffer apoplectic seizures because the air in Swanage costs 10p more than the air in Weymouth.

Suddenly, boats cost the earth. And even when you've bitten the bullet, doubled the branch subs, flogged off all the kit that wasn't nailed down, and raised the deposit on the bloody thing, that's when your troubles really begin.

First there's the trailer. This has to be hand-built, apparently, by rocket scientists from NASA, from girders of freeze-hardened tungsten steel.

Then there are the engines. At least two, each weighing several tonnes and packing more power than *Bluebird*. Long gone are the days when you started your outboard with a piece of string which inevitably snapped on the third pull and sent you cannoning down the length of the boat like a circus entertainer.

Now each of your engines needs two slightly smaller engines to turn it over – and these small engines require four even smaller engines, and so on.

Enough hydraulic gear to embarrass a JCB sighs and whines in the stern, programmed to lift the giant engines when the satellite navigation system identifies land within five nautical miles (your new RIB draws around 6m).

Apart from the nav system, the boat carries a magnetometer powerful enough to pinpoint a 1950 farthing at the bottom of the Marianas Trench; a directional geigercounter for carbon-dating flotsam and jetsam; a UNIX-based minicomputer with a relational database carrying details of more than a million individual molluscs and crustaceans (socio-economic background, current income, personal tastes and preferences, etc); a Super Nintendo; and a McDonalds.

But for all this technology, it seems to me that the fun has gone out of dive boating. Never again will we sit, up to our waists in water, singing sea shanties as three hopeless incompetents dismantle the engine and toss the important bits into Loch Sunart.

Never again will we have to keel-haul Arthur "Blinky" Birkinshaw for driving the 5m Avon up Lulworth Beach and into the lounge of The Flatulent Monk.

Never again will Hamish Lumsden drive us to the wreck of the *James Eagan Layne* and drop us, with unerring accuracy, in 3m of lifeless slime where the monotony is relieved only by the jagged shards of lavatory bowls and the occasional live artillery shell.

The simple inflatable was navigation's answer to the pac-a-mac. With its passing, something beautiful and valuable has disappeared forever.

Let's hear it for beekeepers and dilettantes!

THE BRITISH Sub-Aqua Club has a fight on its hands. Like so many of this nation's great institutions, its very foundations are being attacked by Outsiders – diabolical, scheming foreigners, intent on rationalising diving and making it productive and cost effective and service orientated.

The time has come to stop the rot. We experienced divers must stand up and be counted. "Enough," we must cry. "Thus far and no further! If the Almighty had meant diving clubs to be cost effective, he'd have created Treasurers who were familiar with the concept of double-entry book keeping!"

What is happening to our great Club would not be tolerated elsewhere in our society.

Imagine the uproar if the Americans tried to replace the monarchy with a Professional Association of Hereditary Rulers. The consequences would be unthinkable. Before long they'd be selling advance copies of the Queen's Speech to the tabloids and charging the public to look around Buckingham Palace...

We Britons would never stand for it.

Why, then, have we allowed the blight of Professionalism to taint that other pillar of national tradition, the BSAC?

But wait, you cry. Hold! On the contrary, we have risen magnificently to the PADI challenge. Have we not progressively augmented the price of novice training over the past 10 years, so that it now costs almost as much to be trained by British amateurs as by American professionals?

It's a start, I admit. But, as usual, we're moving neither far nor fast enough.

Why does it still take us weeks to train a diver? Why can't we do it in a morning?

It really would be very simple: distribute a few leaflets on Sennen beach, and round up a bunch of likely punters.

Then a quick five minutes on Boyle's Law, mask clearing and the "I am out of air" signal, and shove 'em off the back of a 4m workboat into 30m of black ice off the Longships. Bingo! Fifty quid, straight on to the branch bottom line.

If it's progress, maybe we should invite it in before it kicks down the door.

On the other hand, perhaps it's already too late. Perhaps we shouldn't try to beat the Yanks at their own game. Perhaps it's time we asserted ourselves, consolidated, built upon the strengths that made the BSAC the envy of the diving world.

Perhaps we should launch the Part-time Lackadaisical Organisation of Dilettantes and Imposters (PLODI). This would represent, if you like, the full-blooded expression of those sacred principles that lie at the very heart of the BSAC philosophy.

The organisation would be divided into branches, each located at, and named after, a public house. Such a system would far better reflect the prime interest of the average British diver than does the present one, which uses as its point of focus a swimming-pool or lecture facility.

The key offices in the branch would fall to those who drew the shortest straw. This would replace the BSAC system in which the

PLODI

posts of Branch Diving Officer, Secretary, Chairman, *et al*, are given automatically to anyone who bothers to turn up at the AGM.

Statistically, the proposed "blind lottery" electoral system is likely to produce a far greater degree of expertise among branch officers than the present one. Some adjustments, then, may have to be made to ensure that the character of the committee is not distorted by anything resembling competence.

There's nothing new in this, of course. Why, my own branch of the BSAC has successively elected as Equipment Officer a poet, a demolition contractor and a beekeeper.

True to the ancient traditions of the Mother Club, PLODI will endeavour to keep the diving to a minimum.

Inevitably, a few genuine enthusiasts are bound to slip through the net, and these will almost certainly suggest pool sessions, trips to the coast and similar unpleasantnesses.

However, their worst excesses can be countered with those time-honoured BSAC techniques – the three-year Novice training course, the seized outboard and the dreadful long-range weather forecast.

Used skilfully, these can be combined to keep all but the most tiresome and energetic members safely ensconced in the bar.

As we seasoned veterans are so acutely aware, there's no enthusiasm like the enthusiasm of the new recruit. PLODI will do all it can to divert, dampen and discourage this sort of unseemly excitation before it develops into the full-blown Keenness syndrome.

Certain strategies have always proved highly effective in this area, such as keeping the lecture timetable flexible so that a repeat of last week's lecture can be substituted at short notice for this week's, to prevent any unwanted progress in the Novice's training.

Or ensuring that the number of instructors is maintained at an absolute minimum, and that every qualified teacher suffers from a recurring back injury, migrainous headaches, or some other debilitating complaint.

In short, then, PLODI will succeed in fending off the scourge of commercialism.

And it is in my customary spirit of modest and disinterested selflessness that I humbly offer myself as the organisation's President For Life.

Anything goes
by mail order

WITH THE possible exceptions of nuclear fission and the latex prophylactic, nothing has so shaped our century as Mail Order. It has opened a Pandora's Box, empowering us to make real our wildest fantasies.

In the old days, our worst excesses of whimsy were constrained by sheer practicality. A pair of motor car slippers with illuminating headlamps might have seemed a good idea while you dozed before a coal fire after a couple of bottles of sweet British sherry.

But the idea would lose much of its sparkle as you waited in the rain for the 53 bus that would take you to Morrish & Sons' nightwear department to buy them.

Today, all you have to do is scribble down your credit card number on a form, and after 28 days (allowing for packing and postage) the awful slippers will magically appear.

Only this morning, I was offered a vacuum cleaner for use on household pets; a device for turning broken bottles into water tumblers; the chance to develop stomach muscles like Jean-Claude Van Damme; and a kite that takes aerial photographs of your home.

It goes without saying that cheap gimmickry of this sort appeals only to the bored and gullible masses who will fritter away what little discretionary income they may command upon useless trinkets and gadgets.

At least we have been spared some of the excesses that have proliferated in America (birthplace of mail order). While in Texas recently, I thumbed through a copy of Soldier of Fortune – a magazine aimed at vigilantes, serial killers and psychopathic combat veterans.

After articles with titles like Creative Knife Fighting and The Garrotte: Functional or Fun? were ten, solid pages of mail order. Here you could send for anything from a replica gun to a real grenade launcher, a Malaysian kukri to a decommissioned submarine.

But what really caught my eye was an ad that read:

"Own A Genuine Timber Wolf. German Shepherds are for cissies, Rottweilers are for wimps; strut your stuff with the Real Thing – a genuine, full-blood Montana Timber Wolf. Only $159.95 (inc p&p) or $299.95 for two."

In Britain, we still maintain a modicum of restraint. But I can't suppress a shiver of apprehension as I watch the advance of mail order in the pages of the diving press.

Selecting a random issue of DIVER, I note that I could order a fossilised shark's tooth, a 6m "unsinkable" dory (I love a challenge), a diving trip to Disneyland, and a woman.

Actually, I couldn't have ordered the woman – she was looking for a "scrumptious diving instructor, under 35" to help her "take the plunge". While I am widely acknowledged as scrumptious, I'm a little past the sell-by date.

The fascination of mail order lies in the promise of a bargain. What wonders are hiding there between the bland, grey lines of print?

"Don't Miss the Match! Submarine colour TV, guaranteed reception to 300m. All channels including Sky via all-new water-orbiting 'Saturite'. Batteries, wrist-strap and five-mile cable attachment extra."

And the only thing that stops you buying the first diving holiday you come to is the second diving holiday, then the third:

"Learn to Dive in Tierra del Fuego. You don't have to go to the ends of the Earth to learn to dive. But what the hell? Prevailing Force 9 gales, freak storms, sub-zero water temps, nil viz, thick fog, ice floes, grim accommodation, terrible food. Perfect introduction to British diving."

But beware – small ads can often slip through the net of the Advertising Standards Authority. Precisely because they're small, they're often less "honest, decent and truthful" than the consumer has a right to expect.

"Dive St Mungo. Completely unexploited Hebridean island, clear water, unusual marine life, incredible drop-offs. A diving holiday you'll never forget."

On the face of it, an alluring prospect. But what the ad doesn't tell you is that St Mungo has been deserted since 1939, when the MoD used it as a testing ground for the Morg's Syndrome bacterium. Basically it's hard to know what to do with an island covered by 6m toxic buttercups and prowled by two-headed carnivorous sheep.

To describe the water as clear is technically correct. It is completely clear of fish, for a start. The few unfortunate cod that strayed within 5 miles of St Mungo were removed by remotely controlled robots from fish and chip shops in the North West, and are now encased forever in lead-lined cannisters in tunnels beneath Ben Nevis.

The term "unusual marine life" probably refers to the sea cucumber known to local fishermen as Auld McNab. This freakish 20m invertebrate became the first example of the class Holothuroidea to complete an Open University degree in Business Administration, and recently applied for a grant from the Scottish Office to open a secretarial college for molluscs.

Unhappily, the phrase "incredible drop-offs" is almost certainly a tasteless reference to the medical problems experienced by members of the BSAC's Sutton Coldfield branch in the months following their ill-advised St Mungo Expedition of 1993.

But such cynical abuses aside, Mail Order can be a useful and flexible shopping medium for the busy diver. What better way to obtain your silver-style medallion commemorating the opening by Her Majesty, Queen Elizabeth the Queen Mother of the new compressor at Whitley Bay?

Or your 100:1 scale sculpture depicting the sinking of the freighter Billy Boy off Beachy Head in 1931, lovingly crafted in finest lead-crystal glass with an engraved inscription by DIVER's Kendall McDonald?

Or, indeed, your copy of Blackford's Diving Life and Times, the hilarious first volume by diving's master wit which earned the tumultuous approbation of critic and adoring public alike?

Credit cards at the ready, friends.

Are you receiving me?

"ONE DAY SOON," enthused Roy Smallpage in a recent issue of DIVER, "divers will be able to speak to each other under water, and to their surface party, and beyond."

Forgive me, but I don't understand. Why should divers want to speak to each other? I can't imagine anything worse. For me, one of the great advantages of getting into the water is not having to speak to divers. Or anybody else.

Imagine: there you are, off Cape Drear in the Farthest Hebrides in 30m of heaving, freezing slime. Suddenly, for one magical instant, the fog of sediment clears and you glimpse The Galleon – bolt upright on the sea bed, spar and bulwark intact, the tatters of her 500-year-old sails still flapping in the Gulf Stream, and cascades of glittering Spanish doubloons spilling from her ruptured holds into the sand.

Suddenly, a crackle from your multi-frequency noise-cancelling voice-activated personal communications module. It's your wife. "Ah, there you are! Where have you been? I've been trying to get you for hours. If you must go off with that wretched club of yours instead of mowing the lawn like you promised faithfully you would, you might at least stay in touch. Anything could have happened. The house could have burned down. Mother could have had one of her turns. Anyway, listen, I want you to stop off at the Spar on the way home and get me a large pack of disposable nappies – the pink ones, not the blue ones you bought last time (honestly, sometimes I think you live in a dream world). Now don't forget. And you'll have to put your skates on – they close at 5 o'clock on a Saturday."

As for being able to talk to your buddy, that's also a luxury I can do without...

"This is Colin to Andy, Colin to Andy, are you receiving me?"

"Yes Colin. What is it?"

"Colin to Andy. I've just been thinking, it must be very strange indeed being a fish."

"I'm sorry?"

"Colin to Andy. Yeah, well, I know it sounds a bit funny, but I'm serious. I mean, they're actual, living life forms, right? They've got brains and bones and things, right? And yet we can't sort of imagine what it's like to *be* them. Sort of."

"I'm not sure I get your drift, Colin. Exactly what are you on about?"

"Well, I mean, they're not like *us*, are they? They don't, say, read newspapers, or sing, or anything. And I mean, they're all the same. You don't get one fish that's good at one thing, like golf, say, and another fish that's no good at golf, but *is* good at something else. Like chess. That's really weird, don't you think? Over."

"I can safely say that it's never really occurred to me, Colin."

"Sorry to have bothered you. I was just thinking, that's all."

"That's perfectly all right, Colin. Over and out."

"Ten four."

(Thirty seconds later.)

"Colin to Andy, Colin to Andy. Are you receiving me?"

"Colin – you see that person next to you? The one who's about to beat your brains out with the pipe wrench? Well, that's me. So that if I weren't receiving you, it would be a fairly damning indictment of modern information technology, wouldn't it?"

"I was just going to say – it must be even weirder, being a winkle..."

Of course, as in all things, as in life itself, the picture isn't entirely black. I can see some marginal advantages to being able to communicate freely under water.

Placing that last-minute bet on Policeman's Helmet in the 2.30 at Doncaster, for instance. Ordering the motor car bedroom slippers with the illuminating headlamps from your Options catalogue.

After all, there's a lot of "dead time", even on the most interesting dive – time when you could usefully be dealing with petty domestic chores. I recall how, while diving the remains of the Japanese Imperial Fleet in Truk Lagoon, I used two tin cans linked by 60m of cotton (a primitive forerunner of the modern radio link) to alter my standing order to British Gas in Bournemouth.

But such advantages must be of marginal interest to your average diver. Far more significant are the improvements to diving safety conferred by better communications.

"No longer," eulogises Smallpage, "will novices be left to suffer their mute loneliness at a time when they really need audible as well as visual reassurance."

You're relaxing at home, listening to Askenase playing Beethoven's piano sonatas when the phone rings...

"Hello, can I speak to Mister Blackford please?"

"This is he."

"Hello, Mister Blackford. I don't know if you remember me, but you took me for my Sports Diver last April. Angus McIlrath?"

"Er... I'm just trying to think..."

"Quite small? Reddish hair? My grandad did the stained glass for Ripon Cathedral?"

"Um, well, I'm sure I'd remember you if I saw you, Angus. But what can I do for you?"

"I wonder if you could give me a bit of advice."

"I'll do my best. Where are you speaking from?"

"I'm on the wreck of *The Pantomime Horse*. You know, near Land's End. In Cornwall."

"Good heavens! What are you doing there?"

"Waiting for my buddy. That's Norman. You know – tall? Slightly balding?"

"Where is he?"

"I don't know. Gone up, I expect. He was running out of air 20 minutes ago."

"How's *your* air?"

"Five bars left."

"Well, why don't *you* go up, too?"

"I can't. My foot's stuck in this net thing."

"This is TERRIBLE! What can I do?"

"Well, as I said, I was wondering if you could give me some advice. By the way, I'm really sorry to bother you at home, but…"

"Quickly, man! What do you need to know?"

"Just remind me – what's the signal for 'diver in need of assistance'?"

CLUB TIMES

The illustrious annals of Sturminster Parva Branch

"When our daughter announced that she was 'in the club' I thought she'd joined Sturminster Parva branch. Thank God she was only pregnant."

John Bantin, DIVER Magazine

20 years in the branch pool

IT'S A long time since I learned to dive. To give you some idea of just how long, Africa was still joined to South America, and Mike Todd took a Medium in wetsuits.

Things were very different then. To start with, every BSAC Diver was over 40. This was because it took 20 years just to qualify as a Novice.

This seems astonishing in hindsight, but it was that sort of thoroughness and attention to detail that won us our reputation as the best divers in the world.

The system was ruthless and gruelling. The course began with a test of initiative and determination that would have scared off 2 Para.

You had to get from the Bricklayer's Arms in Portman Square to the branch pool in Seymour Place before 7pm on a Friday night.

Since you didn't get to the Bricklayer's until 5.30, you could hardly leave before 6.55. Which gave you just five minutes to jog the 200 yards to the pool, encumbered by fins, mask, snorkel, towel and six pints of Speer and Himmler's Weapons' Grade Lager.

If you were so much as a minute late, TJ was already teaching and you'd have to come back next week. If you were on time, TJ wasn't teaching that night and you'd have to come back next week.

If you came back next week, it was a pity you hadn't turned up last week, because TJ had hung around for you until 7.30 and you weren't exactly flavour of the month, they could tell you.

This was called the F test, for reasons which are not difficult to imagine. Once you passed it, you were invited to enter the water for the A test. For a first-hand account of this notorious initiation ordeal, we need look no further than the log-book of noviciate diver Nigel Fishwick, of Sturminster Parva branch:

"Until today, I thought an A test was a nuclear explosion of an awesome destructive power that could reduce mountains to dust, turn dust to glass and extinguish all plant and animal life over a radius of 20 miles.

"Little did I suspect that the BSAC has developed a weapon more terrifying by far. An ordeal that can break the heart and spirit of a man like a bear breaks a toothpick. (Note: probably a reference to the Nordic diver-poet, Grimdyke Thorgrimmsun, much read at the time: "It is a brave man who picks his teeth in company with a bear." – Ed.)

"First you must swim 20 lengths of the pool, backwards. To propel oneself feet first through the water in this way is exhausting in the extreme. But worse is to follow. The candidate must repeat the exercise blindfold while wearing a brass skirt. This is designed to simulate as precisely as possible the experience of diving in the English Channel.

"Next comes the Solo Synchronised Swimming, which involves standing on one's head in the deep end while the instructor slips into the oxygen rebreather cupboard for a cigarette. Then it's into the pyjamas and out to the brick pond to recover the tractor parts.

"Apparently, it's all about Water Confidence and the atrocious conditions that divers encounter in British waters. If you can raise a two-hundredweight differential in 60ft of freezing pit spoil at night, wearing only winceyette jim-jams, then you'll have a fighting chance when it comes to a 20ft shore dive at Redcar in late July.

"Lastly, there's the hated Memory test. This is loosely based on *Bruce Forsyth's Generation Game*. The instructor shows you a set of diving kit, piece by piece, and you try to commit it to memory. Then you pretend you're going diving and you tell him what items he should pack in your bag. I forgot the mask and the boots but my instructor let me off.

"Many qualified divers even forget their wallets in their rush to reach the dive-site, he said; and a famous National Instructor once drove to Penzance without his drysuit. (Fishwick's account does not name this individual. Any assistance from the Reader would be gratefully received. In fact, memory problems are so common among divers that the phenomenon has attracted the interest of the medical world – see "The Lost Weekend" by Dr P Wilmshurst, *The Lancet* in May (or was it June?) nineteen-fifty-something or other, when Wilmshurst recounts the strange case of Havant Branch, who once put to sea without their boat. – Ed.)

"The A test completed, it's time for the Medical. Candidates must produce some evidence of a liver and must weigh less than the Club van. A chest X-ray may be requested by the Diving Officer, to establish the existence of a chest in cases where the upper thorax is concealed by chins. The smoking of tobacco is permitted, but the Club recommends a safe daily upper limit of 200 full-strength Capstans. While consumption in excess of this limit may not affect the diver's physical performance, it can result in ecological damage to the coastal area through acid rain.

"This is 1957, after all."

But it was the lectures that really set the BSAC apart from other diving authorities. Who else would insist that before you set foot in the water you should learn the Gas Laws, conversational Urdu and the principles of thermodynamics while demonstrating a detailed knowledge of the early films of Wim Wenders, cooking with yoghurt, and the life and works of Lancelot T Spottiswode, inventor of the self-watering bean?

Undoubtedly, it is thanks to the emphasis placed by the BSAC upon this theoretical training that the British diver can explain the incidence of negative causality in sub-particle physics, but couldn't find the *Lusitania* in a Jacuzzi.

And so, two decades had passed when I finally rolled backwards off the tube of the 4m club inflatable half a mile off Fowey.

Twenty years of hard work and dedication, disappointment and frustration, punctuated by moments of illumination – the pride of achievement, the thrill that accompanies the greatest discovery of all. The discovery of oneself.

Thanks to the Club I had a Master's Degree in Organic Chemistry, I held the Brunel Chair of Engineering at Yale University, and I was fluent in 12 languages including Dogan, which consists entirely of whistling sounds produced in the nasal passages.

How irritating, then, that I should merely float on the surface like a great inflatable whale – having forgotten my weightbelt.

A big night
for the Branch

IT'S DOWNRIGHT peculiar. Watch the Branch on the beach, or in the boat, or in the car park, and they look like divers. All of them. Even the most hideously misshapen of them, those with the most grotesquely distended bellies; those with the cratered thighs of cellulite sumo wrestlers; those with buttocks like globulous pendules of candle fat, set to drip ripely upon a priceless rug – they still retain a kind of rough dignity.

They are the Aquanauts, after all, those of clenched jaw and steely eye, determined to endure Nature's harshest insults if it should grant them even a glimpse of that Forbidden World beneath the billows.

But encounter them at the Branch annual dinner and dance at the Sir Oswald Mosley Assembly Rooms, Sturminster Parva, and it's a very different story.

Alf's cummerbund is so spleen-rupturingly tight that his lower bowel is threatening to obstruct his oesophagus. Alf's wife has been poured into a little black dress that might have come from the condom machine in a Bangkok gay bar.

Colin Mouldey is plastered because the bar was free until seven. After six pints of Barsted's Old Chesil Skeg Mangler in 40 minutes, he sways like a fibreglass boat aerial in a stiff breeze. He has attached himself like a limpet to Desmond, mainly because, after five months of painful and embarrassing rebuttals, Desmond has finally managed to corner Lisette, the Branch Beauty from Krakow in Poland.

Lisette has grace, poise and a lithe sensuality that looks even better in the Sir Oswald Mosley Rooms than it does on Swanage Pier. She is the granddaughter of a dispossessed Polish count, and

took an effortless First in post-Cartesian philosophy at the
Sorbonne between modelling for Helmut Newton in Italian *Vogue*.

"Eh!" barks Colin, blank eyes, fishy grin. "Eh 'ello, *gor*-juss!
Aryavinag'time, eh? Jewannadrink? Eh? Lissen! Lissen t'thissun!
Na, na, *lissen*! Issa good'n, isthiss:

How d'ye know if yer wife's dead?"

With wild eyes, Lisette beseeches Desmond to rescue her.
After five fruitless months, this was Desmond's heaven-sent
chance.

He blew it.

He could have rescued Lisette from the appalling Colin and
won her undying gratitude, but he didn't – because in the final
analysis, even more than he wanted Lisette, he wanted to hear the
punchline of Colin's joke.

He was a diver, you see.

"C'mon!" croaked Colin. *"How d'ye know if yer wife's dead?"*

"I don't know," replied the beautiful philosophy graduate
miserably. "How *do* you?"

"Sex is the same," howled the triumphant Colin, *"but the
ironin' mounts up!"*

The Master of Ceremonies is a tiny, spherical person in a
bursting red uniform jacket. His voice is like Whitby foghorn.

"Ladies and gentle*men*! Pray take your seats for dinner!"

The rank and file of Sturminster Parva Branch drift from the
bar into the Goebbels Room, where they are herded to their seats
by a platoon of crisp-pinnied waitresses, not one of them under 60.

As Lisette is finally saved from Colin by the seating plan, he
shouts across the tables to her, "D'yer gerrit? Eh? D'yer?"

"Pray be upstanding," booms the MC, "for your President,
your Chairman and your Committee!"

Led by Alf and Mrs Alf, the Branch brass shuffle in, self-
consciously, to the traditional slow hand clap of the membership.
The sound system blares out Beethoven's *Ode to Joy*, the personal
choice of Mrs Alf. Ideally, she'd have gone for *The Ride of the
Valkyrie*, but Alf had put his foot down on that one.

President of the Branch is Carlton McKenzie, one of its
founders and a member for 28 years. He is accompanied by… by…
who knows? The membership has long since lost count of the slim,
athletic blondes in sequined sheaths slashed to the waist who

95

giggle and simper at Carlton's side at such functions.

Then there's Eric Smith, Training Officer. That must be his wife – but the more observant will note that he studiously avoids the eyes of Desirée Silke-Sheere, newly qualified Sport Diver, as he passes her table.

Next comes Norris Napier, Branch Treasurer. Somehow, Norris never found the time to marry. As always, he has brought his mother, although she must be 90.

Then there are Derek and Maisie, Branch Secretary and spouse. Maisie sweeps into the room with a great rustling of satin, like the wind in the sails of a galleon, while Derek bobs cheerfully at her stern, like a tender.

They are followed by Dilly Jobbins, the newly elected Diving Officer, and her friend Maxine, a judo instructor with the military police.

Next Eric Jones, Equipment Officer. Jones the Gear. He has a dishevelled air about him, as if until five minutes ago he was reproofing the underside of the Zodiac. His big hands, robbed of anything to dismantle or clean or connect, fumble awkwardly with each other.

His dinner jacket looks as though it was fired at him from a great distance. There are odd bulges about the pockets – compressor parts, probably, brought along in case he has a minute or two between courses to check them over.

Laurie Mack, Social Secretary, brings up the rear, accompanied by his fiancée and by Tony Blandford, the diving writer and Guest of Honour at tonight's dinner.

The High Table fills up and the chatter is cut short by the MC. "Pray silence as your Chairman reads the Diver's Prayer!"

Now the brigade of waitresses creaks arthritically into action, whacking down the prawn salads with a sound like small arms fire. No sooner does mayonnaise smear chin than the MC bangs the table.

He peers through bottle-bottom glasses at a scrap of paper. "Mister Kevin Muldoon wishes to take wine with the Kamikaze Trouser Lobsters of Loch Sunart – and especially the Brasso Boys of the *Dunsinane!*"

This is greeted with raucous laughter and cheering by all except Tony Blandford, for whom the toast might as well have been the instructions for a Martian lawnmower.

He grins amiably, nevertheless, and drains his glass of medium sweet Lambrusco.

BY 'ECK, that's a lovely drop of wine, is that," opines Laurie Mack, Social Secretary and self-styled *bon viveur*. "Very drinkable indeed."

Tony Blandford clears his throat. "Yes, that's a rather odd expression, I always think, 'drinkable'."

Laurie glances uncertainly at his Guest of Honour. "How do you mean?"

"Well, what are you going to do with a bottle of wine other than drink it?" Blandford stares thoughtfully into his glass of medium sweet Lambrusco. "Though actually, you could use this one to ice a cake."

"Ha! That's good is that! Ice a cake!" Blandford is making the Social Sec nervous.

"Still," muses the Guest of Honour in the same dreamy tone, "it's better than the Angolan Beaujolais they served at Stockton Branch last month. You could have restored masonry with that. It's the first wine I've ever known to carry a Haz Chem warning. It was first imported under special licence by the Atomic Energy Authority, apparently, for the treatment of spent fuel rods."

Now Laurie is out of his depth. "Is that true?"

"Perfectly," replies Blandford, draining his glass.

"Well... by 'eck!"

The MC crashes his gavel on the table. "Mrs Nadine Bonsor would like to take wine with Big Boy Bruce and the Challaborough Chippendales!" (Howls of helpless laughter all round.)

Blandford yawns and pushes back his chair. "Ah, well! Coffee's coming, I suppose I'd better go and write my speech."

"Ha, ha!" barks Laurie "Very good! Write your speech!"

"No, really, I'm serious. I have enormous faith in the power of spontaneity. Don't you?"

With a sinking heart, Laurie Mack watches his Guest of Honour weave unsteadily towards the bar with a pencil, a paper napkin and half a bottle of warm, white wine. These celebrity types were all the same. Oh yes, they're so very smart and comical when you see them on TV, or read their bloody columns in the magazines. But meet them in real life, and they're walking nightmares. Drunks, drug addicts and perverts, the lot of 'em. "Oh, Lord, what have I done?" he mutters.

The lounge is practically deserted. A barman in a crumpled waistcoat empties the brimming ashtrays into a plastic bucket.

Blandford settles himself at a small table in the corner and takes a long pull at the Lambrusco. What should it be tonight, then? He'd better not risk the one about New Labour repealing the Gas Laws. It would go straight over their heads...

"Hey! Here, mate! It is, isn't it...?" Colin lurches across the lounge to Blandford's table, an Embassy Regal in one hand and a pint of Barsted's Old Chesil Skeg Mangler in the other. "By God, it is! I've seen your picture in the DIVER, mate! Don't tell... na, don't... you're Sir Bernard Eaton! 'Ere, I always read your bit – about the wrecks an' that. An' when you test out the weightbelts, an' that."

Blandford stares stonily at the grinning intruder, willing him to go away, but it's no good. Colin drags up a chair and bangs down his pint, spilling half of it over Blandford's notes.

He leers and winks, "'Ere, Sir Bernard, whassit like, then, gettin' all them birds to try on the wetsuits? Eh? Nice work if you can gerrit is what I say, an' good bloody luck to yer, mate. Lissen, I'm not one o' them bloody spoilsports, y'know – if you get to go off to desert islands with beautiful birds *and* keep all the kit, well, it's no skin off my nose."

"Bernard Eaton is in fact the publisher of DIVER magazine," replies Blandford levelly, "and as far as I'm aware, the honour of a knighthood has so far eluded him.

"The 'wrecks an' that', as you so quaintly dub the historical and wreck diving section of the magazine, is written by Kendall McDonald, while the equipment tests are conducted, generally speaking, by John Bantin, who takes his work extremely seriously and, for the record, does not get to 'keep the kit'.

"Which brings us to me. I am Tony Blandford. I write the humorous article at the back of the magazine, entitled *Coma Position*. I would be surprised if my work featured in your monthly repertoire of reading matter, since it usually consists of a thousand words, strung together in what we writers call 'sentences', some of them even longer than 'Last orders'."

But even this leaden irony fails to penetrate the armour of Colin's inebriation. He just winks and grins fishily at a point 1m behind Blandford's head. "Fair dues, Saint Bernard! Y'can trust me, my lips are sealed, mate! 'Ere, *how d'you know if your wife's dead?*"

Blandford hazards a guess: "She's prepared to lie in the same bed as *you?*"

"Eh! Eh! That was very sharp, was that! Very clever! You didn't get to be a lord for nothin' did yer? But I'll tell yer anyway. Ready? *Sex is the same, but the ironin' mounts up!*"

Meanwhile, on high table, Alf leans over to Mrs Alf. "Where's the speaker, pet? He's on in two minutes, and I don't like to worry poor Laurie, what with him only burying his missus last week."

"It's all right, Hubby. Here he comes now. Goodness, he looks a bit the worse for wear…"

Tony Blandford collapses into his seat, and stares helplessly at his notes. Colin's beer has reduced them to a misty blur, which is more or less echoed by the state of his brain.

"Ad lib, old boy," he mutters. "It won't be the first time."

"… a hearty welcome to our Guest of Honour, Mister Tony Blandford!"

He drags himself to his feet with a gargantuan effort and surveys the expectant, smiling audience.

"Than' you, everybody, than' you Laurie! Now then: *How d'you know if your wife's dead?*"

Stalled on the starting grid

A LITTLE knot of divers gazed at the new notice in the compressor room.

Hi guys, it's get off your bottom time again!
Let out those Long Johns and dust off those DVs!
Let's set our phasers to 'Sun'
and head west down old Route 3 to Weymouth City!
That's right – Weymouth, so good they named it!
Davy says, Let's Go DIVING!
David Denge Diving Officer

"Dave," observed Tony Blandford quietly, "you are the sort of person who can make a mild-mannered fellow like myself take up an automatic weapon and murder a coach load of drum majorettes."

"Hah! That's good is that, Tone! Drum majorettes!"

Involuntarily, Tony squeezed his bag of porky scratchings until they were reduced to a handful of pig dust.

Forget the neutron bomb, forget germ warfare. If it were only slightly infectious, such indefatigable good nature as Dave Denge's would destroy the planet in a day.

Nevertheless, Blandford had to admit, he was right about one thing. The start of the diving season was alarmingly close. He really ought to sort himself out.

Ruefully, he recalled his good intentions of the previous October. How he'd vowed to powder his drysuits and put his bottle in for test, so that it wouldn't be a nerve-racking ordeal in the spring.

Hmm. Here it was, April, and his nerves were already racked. He couldn't even remember what he'd done with his kit for the winter. He had a dim folk-memory that the potting shed might have been involved in some way.

Next day, Tony Blandford rose early. Still half asleep, he stumbled down to the shed and prised open the door. He was almost knocked flat by a flock of greater horseshoe bats, which fled flapping and blind into the spring sunshine.

Inside, the air was heavy with damp and decay. He might have been a tomb robber, penetrating the inner sanctum of a pyramid.

On the worm-eaten floor was a shapeless, stinking mound, iced with a greasy patina of green and white bat droppings. He had an awful intuition that this must be his dive bag.

* * * * * * * * *

"Exactly how long is it since your last medical, Mr Blandford?" enquired the doctor. "I can't seem to erase this mental picture I have of you in flares and a kipper tie."

"Ah yes. That would be right. 1972, give or take. I've been living... abroad... since then. You see.

"Oh, really? How interesting. Where?"

"Where? Oh, *where*! Yes. Er, Runcorn."

"Runcorn, Cheshire?"

"Yes, that's the blighter! Well, ha, it's more abroad than Reading, isn't it? Ha!"

"Well, I'm not sure why you have no discernible hint of a medical record, Mister Blandford. You're going to need a chest X-ray. I'll book you in for a week Wednesday."

"No good, I'm afraid. I'm diving at the weekend."

"I wouldn't."

"What? Why not?"

"I wouldn't enjoy it. I can't swim, for one thing."

"No, I mean, is there any reason why *I* shouldn't dive?"

"Several. The cold, the impenetrable darkness, the absence of any marine life form larger than a planktonic hydroid. How's that for a start?"

"No I..."

"Then there are one's fellow divers – animals, almost without exception. Loud, aggressive animals to boot, out of whose backsides, if they are to be believed, there shines a universe of suns."

"I..."

"The weather, of course, does little to enhance the experience. Did you know that during the month of July 1997 it was actually wetter above water in Lulworth than it was below? Of course, it wouldn't really matter if one could retire to an intimate, comfortably appointed restaurant to ride out the storm over a dish of local, freshly caught *fruits de mer* and a cold bottle of honest Chablis. But, instead, one is condemned to a microwaved pastie and a chipped mug of lukewarm tea with the bag still in it, surrounded by baying, snotty infants and feral wasps in a Portakabin with a sandy lino floor and air thick with the stink of gaberdine and the plastic hats of sad Inland Revenue clerks from Penge. I could go on."

"No! No, please don't. I get your drift. But what I really meant was, is there any medical reason why I shouldn't dive?"

"Oh, I see. Well, nothing specific, I suppose. Frankly, you look a bit of a wreck. I mean, for you to go diving would be a bit like putting to sea in an old coble that's been beached for 10 years. Bit of an act of faith. I mean, it could be perfectly alright. On the other hand, it could sink like a stone. It's very hard to predict that sort of thing."

* * * * * * * * *

"Ah, yes. Mister Blandford, innit? Yeah, well, I'm afraid your bottle's failed its test, mate."

"What? It can't have. There must be some mistake. Why, I only bought it... (some rapid calculations) 12 years ago. No wait – 13."

"That would explain the advanced age of the mice that was livin' in it, then, sir."

"You're kidding?"

"Yes, sir. But, quite honestly, I wouldn't feel safe keepin' flowers in it. We serviced your DV, too. My word, that's a period piece, is that. We 'ad Kendall McDonald in the other day. When he saw your valve, 'e wanted to do one of 'is articles on it. You know – Great Wrecks. I 'ad to wrestle it off 'im I did."

* * * * * * * * *

It had taken Tony Blandford four hours to chip through the granite-like crust of bat dung that encased his dive bag. It hadn't been worth it.

The contents were welded together in an amalgam of rust and sea salt. They came out in one big, spiky chunk, like a Constructivist sculpture, or the dentist's tools from the *Mary Rose*.

Exhausted, he sat down on the lawn and stared at his drysuit. Idly, he brushed at a cobweb on the neck seal.

It stuck to his fingers. He drew back his hand and the latex extruded into long, sticky strings, like the cheese on a black rubber pizza.

"I hate diving," he said.

In search of
fish and felines

NORMAN WELCH couldn't stop diving. It was neither a hobby, nor a sport, nor a pastime. It was an addiction, a desperate obsession.

It began when he was but three years old. The little Norman witnessed a gruesome tragedy. Otto, the family cat, having stared at Maureen the goldfish for two years, suddenly plunged his paw into the bowl, scooped up the fish and swallowed it whole.

The fish lodged in Otto's throat and even though Norman's father held up the cat by his tail and beat his back with a rolled-up copy of *Titbits*, Otto only outlived his piscine victim by a matter of seconds.

Norman looked on in mute, wide-eyed horror. He hadn't cared much for the cat, but Maureen was his special friend. They had shared that unique and intimate relationship that can only exist between a boy and his fish.

Doctor von Stroheim, Norman's psychoanalyst, has explained his patient's passion for diving as an expression of his desire to find his lost Maureen.

If that is so, then Norman's compulsion was informed neither by ordinary logic nor by any understanding of natural history. He dived in the Mediterranean, the Caribbean, the Midgeworths' septic tank, the Great Barrier Reef, the Manchester Ship Canal, the sulphur pools of the Chilean tundra, the Maldives and in the River Tees, a little downstream of the ICI Urea Plant's main waste outfall. None of which diverse habitats would possibly have supported the small, freshwater carp from the darts stall at Shaftesbury Fair that was Maureen.

And yet, when has logic ever held sway over the domain of Love?

Norman's driving passion made him an ideal candidate for Sturminster Parva's ill-fated expedition of 1994. Indeed, from that first briefing in the snug of the Cat & Hacksaw, he was unable to talk or think of anything else.

"At ease, ladies and gentlemen. You may smoke. My name is Wilbury-Fawcett. I am a Colonel in the Queen's Own Foot & Mouth, but, for reasons of security, I would prefer it if from now on you were to call me by my code name which is Binky. B-I-N-K-Y. Everybody got that? I used to have trouble remembering it myself so I invented a little phrase to help me: Belittling the Indigenous Nomads of Kazakstan is Aluminium. Anyway my…"

"Sir!"

"Question from the floor! Yes?"

"Two things, sir. Firstly, that doesn't spell 'Binky'. It spells 'Binka'. And secondly, it doesn't make sense. How can an abstract concept like 'belittling' possibly be described in terms of a metal? Surely the whole point of a mnemonic is that its very meaning lends it memorability. If it doesn't mean anything, it's no more memorable than the thing you're trying to remember. Less so, in fact, because it's longer."

"Well spotted, that man! You …"

"I mean, you might as well say, 'Boniface Ink Normality Kolumbus-with-a-K Yelling'. At least it would end in Y."

"Yes, well, I think you've made your point. As a matter of fact, I included the 'aluminium' as a security measure. No point in having a code name that the enemy can remember. But I like your style. Enquiring mind. No harm in that. What's your name?"

"Welch, sir. Norman."

"Good! Why don't…"

"Wenceslas entertains ladies constantly, Horatio."

"Say again?"

"That's my mnemonic, sir. For Welch."

"Right, well, that's enough about names and such for the present. Let's get on with the business at hand. Now I expect you're wondering why I've asked you all here today."

"Is it anything to do with cats, sir? Or fish?"

"There is a connection, yes, Welch, but you're not supposed to know about it. You're just a character in the Last Gasp column.

Only the Reader is supposed to know about the business with the fish, and thence to make certain deductions and inferences. That's how writing works, you see, Welch. Now if I might continue…"

"Sorry, sir."

"…the purpose of this meeting is to recruit members for an expedition. An extremely important expedition which, were it to meet with success, would infinitely enrich our understanding of the natural world, and bring honour and glory to everyone involved in it. I can't exaggerate…"

"Sir!"

"What is it now, Welch?"

"Is it to do with the Advanced Driving Test?"

"No it…"

"A shrew, then? Are there shrews in it? Or is it about hedges?"

"Now look here, Welch. I've already broken an important rule of narrative writing by acknowledging a connection that only the writer and his audience should perceive at this stage. I've hinted that cats and fish may be tangentially involved, and yet here you are, coming back with a lot of silly, random suggestions that have nothing whatsoever to do with the story."

"I'm sorry, sir. It's just that I know I've let the cat out of the bag a bit, sir, pardon the expression, so I was trying to make amends by acting as if I didn't know about the first thing after all, and that really I'm in the dark like everybody else, sir."

"Yes, well, I'm afraid that in literature, as in life, you can't undo what's already been done. And as it is, you've only succeeded in using up all this month's column, and I haven't even announced the purpose of the extremely important expedition."

"Sorry, sir. What is it?"

"Too late, now. Have to wait 'til next month."

NEXT MONTH

THE STORY SO FAR:

Dive addict Norman Welch has volunteered for a diving expedition of such enormous importance that not even its mysterious leader, Colonel Wilbury-Fawcett, has been informed of its destination and objective.

The expedition is the brainchild of some of the world's most secret people. It was secretly conceived at a confidential location in a country, the name of which must, for reasons of secrecy, remain secret.

Last month, we left Norman as the secret briefing neared its climax. Burning issues are about to be resolved. What is the truth behind this most clandestine of diving expeditions? Who is the sinister Professor Z? Why, in order to play golf, is it necessary to dress like Bing Crosby?

Unfortunately, we might as well ask how many grains of sand there are on Weymouth Beach, or why anyone would call a child Cyril. For only last Tuesday, the offices of DIVER were raided by anonymous agents of the top-secret Ministry Of Certain Things.

They confiscated our records (including Mr Eaton's favourite, a rare 78rpm copy of The Laughing Policeman) and forbade me to continue this story until 30 years have elapsed.

When I protested that the story was purely fictional, they replied, "So are we".

And so, in place of the advertised column there follows a short dissertation that I have provocatively entitled:

LOB-STAR WARS

Lulworth Cove, Dorset – 7.45am, 23 July. The honeyed rays of the sun pluck gently at the last, tattered veils of a dawn mist. Little wavelets sigh on shingle: the sea is grey-clear, stirred only by a light swell that sucks and slaps the rocks at the neck of the bay.

This is Hardy Country, and his poet's soul would have sprung like the lark heavenwards on this glorious morning.

"Bastard!" The stillness is broken by the rasp of a sick gearbox. "Bastard! It's completely knackered, is this van. We should donate it to medical science. Or give it to Nobby to keep his stinking bantams in."

"Shurrup whinging and help us blow up the boat. Mayfair Branch'll be here in half an hour and, if we don't get sorted, they'll clean the caff out of bacon sarnies."

And thus swings into action the mighty machine that is Sturminster Parva in dive mode. Boxes, barrels, ropes, bags, buoys and bottles, keels and crates, tumble out of the reeking innards of the ancient van and form a ragged mountain on the shore.

The air rings with shouts and curses and joyful flatulence as our New Age Pirates struggle with foot pumps, wrestle with flaking stringers.

"I can never remember: is it one dollop of two-stroke oil to 20 thingies of petrol or the other way round?"

"Look! There's half a cheese roll stuck in my boot. It must be from last October!"

"This pump's bloody useless. I don't know why we didn't just hire a hard boat."

"This is a hard boat. It's bloody hard to inflate, any road."

"Look at Colin's new goody bag. It's the size of a duvet cover."

"Actually, it's a pair of Nigel's old Y-fronts."

"Is that right? So it came complete with crabs then?"

They were wrong about Mayfair Branch. True to form, the nation's number one divers pitched up at 11.30, following a leisurely breakfast over the Business Section at one of Bournemouth's less vulgar five-star establishments.

Nonchalantly, they reversed their Scammell Geronimo

halftrack on to the beach, demolishing more than half of the exhibits in the Weymouth Lions' Sunshine club annual sandcastle competition.

The wails of distraught children were drowned by the Scammell's twin turbos as it bulldozed *Tirpitz II* into the water.

Tirpitz was unusual among dive boats. Originally commissioned by Idi Amin as a floating menagerie and bordello, she was later refitted by the French Defence Department to conduct educational and public relations visits to the peoples of the South Sea islands. The torpedo tubes and napalm cannon were removed before her sale to Mayfair Branch.

Three hours later, local fishermen's representative, Richard Bleathman, stormed angrily towards the Sturminster Parva divers. "Who's in charge, here?"

"Him over there. He's the DO."

"As far as I'm concerned, he's an SOB. You lot have been takin' our lobsters."

"Bollocks."

"Don't bother denyin' it. We've just found two pots slashed open and a whole catch of lobsters gone."

"Oh, come on! Two lobbies is hardly 'a whole catch'. I mean, if there *were* two, of course. Which is quite likely, after all, given the number of, um... divers in these, er..."

"If it's not enough that you come down here, frightening our women folk with your cussing and your great, hairy arses. You have to steal our livelihood as well."

"That's not fair. It could've been anyone."

"Then how do you explain the diving knife, not six inches from the damaged pot, with *Jerry Mander, Sturminster Parva Branch* engraved on one side, and *Divers Do It With Crustaceans* on the other?"

"Pure coincidence."

"Not to mention the snorkel with the JM monogram, entangled in the line, and the inscription in the white chinagraph on the base of the pot."

"Let me see that:
Whatever the price, whatever the risk,
Jerry likes his lobster bisque.

"Yes. Right. I see what you mean. Mister Bleathman, I wonder if you'd be good enough to take a stroll along the beach with me? I have some information which I think might be of some interest to you."

"Well…"

"You see, our branch of the British Sub-Aqua Club has for many years been in dispute with another Branch – Mayfair Branch. Toffs from London with an eye for a quick buck and fewer morals than there are sperm whales under Swanage pier.

"To put it bluntly, we've been framed. Set up. We're stool pigeons, dupes, the innocent victims of an elaborate confidence trick."

"Now, look…"

"In short, Mister Bleathman, it was Mayfair Branch who stole your two… your lobsters. And with a little ingenuity and your assistance, I think we can recover them for you."

(To be continued)

Mixed gases and alluring artillery shells

THE ANCIENT DIVER shifted comfortably in his overstuffed armchair which, as usual, entirely eclipsed the roaring log fire and cast the snug of the Cat & Hacksaw into a chilly penumbra.

He threw back his shaggy white head, as his old briar expelled a cloud of acrid smoke. (Most people prefer to smoke tobacco, but the Ancient Diver preferred old briar.)

The Branch gathered about his feet, their young, upturned faces rosy in the firelight. He beckoned to Fiona, the Entertainment Officer. "'Ere! Hoy another stab jacket ont' fire, laddie!"

"It's me, Ancient Diver," she replied crisply. "Fiona."

"Aye, I know. Funny name fer a bloke – but nowt surprises me. There used to be a bird in our branch called Stanley. She were a rum 'un, an' no mistake. She were a vetinary nurse, as I recall, in a secure institution fer psychopathic guard dogs...."

"Now, where was I?"

"You hadn't actually begun your story yet, Ancient Diver."

"No, no laddie. I mean, where *was* I? Last night? And whose trousers are these? And how did I get 'ere? And come to that, where *am* I?"

"You're in the Cat, sir," offered Nigel, the Most Eager Novice. "And you're among friends. And may I just say, sir, that we're all looking forward enormously to another of your 'salty tales'. You're under starter's orders, so to speak!"

The Ancient Diver perked up instantly. "Order? Ta, young woman. Mine's a flagon of Curate's Bowel. Failin' that, I suppose a pint of Alzheimer's will 'ave to do.

"Now, where was I?"

"Well, sir, I don't know if it's any help, but when you arrived you were wearing a bee-keeper's helmet and carrying a copy of *Popular Dog Fighting*."

"Nay lass, I don't mean where *was* I. I know exactly where I was. I was out on Grimm Crag with Molly Biggsthorpe and a few of the lads from the Legion. I mean, whereabouts in me *story* was I?"

"I *think*, Ancient Diver, that I overheard you telling someone that you were intending to address us on the subject of Mixed Gas Diving."

The Ancient Diver almost choked on his foaming quart of Alzheimer's.

"What? Ah, humph! Yes, well... 'Course I were, 'course I were. Daft o' me. I'm gettin' so forgettable of late." With knitted brows and a countenance suggesting the most profound contemplation, he stared into the sagging embers of the fire.

"That's right. Mixed gas divin'. I remember mixed gas divin' from... when would it be?... way back..." Then, for a moment, the mists of Time parted to reveal the golden peaks of Memory, and his craggy face was illuminated by a beam of pure enlightenment.

He settled even deeper into his chair.

"It were Nobby Meicher who first come up with the notion. We'd been divin' on the wreck of the *Sir John Bantin* (God rest 'er wormy old spars), and we'd 'ad the divil of a job, tryin' to get the brass from the aft hold. Sixteen-inch artillerary shells it was, I remember – as corroded an' unpredictable as the day they left the production line at the Woolwich Arsenal.

"Nobby was an inventive type, with a restless, rovin' kind of scientifical mind. '*Ancient Diver*,' he says – well, he didn't actually say 'Ancient Diver', 'cos in those days, I wasn't a day over 70. 'Seth,' he says, 'our problem here is that we don't 'ave enough hexplosive to knock a hole in that there magazine. What we want to do is cut through that plate.'

"Well, once we was back on shore, he solved the problem in a flash. Within a couple of years, workin' day and night with his primitive, rat-powered calculator and a chemistry set what was given to 'im by Michael Faraday..."

"Excuse me, Ancient Diver," piped up the Most Eager Novice, "but I'm afraid Faraday was a physicist."

The Ancient Diver fixed him with a withering glare. "I know 'e was, young woman. That's why 'e gave Nobby 'is chemistry set.

"Anyways, Nobby came up with this notion, an' he says to me, 'Seth, I shall call this Mixed Gas Divin', and one day it'll make me famous, you mark my words'.

"Then he showed me 'is contraption. It were two bottles, joined together wi' gaffer tape, one containin' oxygen, one filled wi' acetylene.

"'It doesn't taste marvellous,' he told me, 'an' after a few minutes, you start to see, like imaginery insects. But you get used to it. Thing is, set fire to it when yer down there, straight off yer DV like, an' it'll cut through anything. Just the job fer that there munitions ship.'

"Even though it were January an' the North Sea had been lashed continuous for weeks by Force 9 gales, we set out from Seahouses at midnight in the old branch coble, *Lusitania*. Bit daft, really, looking back. The wreck was off Folkestone.

"Still, with a followin' wind, we made Kent in just under the hour, and moored bang on the wreck site.

"We kitted up as best we could and set about workin' out a dive plan. 'Seth,' says Nobby, 'take my advice and always remember that old diver's adage: plan the dive, and then, in the heat of the moment, completely ignore what you agree and make it up as you go along, based loosely on a folk memory of the tables and the logic of a retarded periwinkle.'

"Within minutes, we'd run through our buddy checks and we were ready to dive on the *Sir John Bantin*. I'll always remember Nobby's last words: 'Seth, mate, soon we'll be down there, slicin' open the powder room of the biggest munitions ship ever built with my patent oxyacetylene torch, so we can get to that allurin' cargo of dangerously unstable high-explosive artillerary shells. Isn't this what diving's all about?'"

The Ancient Diver stared into the fire in silent contemplation.

"And... then?" prompted the Most Eager Novice.

"Hmm? Oh – an' then he lit 'is fag."

A horse called Hannibal

THE CHAIRMAN of the Official Branch Investigatory Committee peered at Colin, our Treasurer, through spectacles like bottle bottoms.

"What fascinates me, Mister Mouldey, is that for a single instant you imagined that holding an international dive show in Sturminster Parva could possibly result in anything other than catastrophic and ruinous failure."

"Well, I s'pose it is fascinatin'," replied Colin helpfully. "It's always the same with disasters. You know, the *R101* an' the *Titanic* an' that. Sad – but fascinatin'."

The Chairman stared even harder at Colin. Was he daring to be facetious while testifying before so solemn an inquiry – and in the light of a financial loss that would almost certainly plunge the Branch into the twilight of eternal bankruptcy?

No, he wasn't. Colin wasn't even aware of the existence of irony. He wouldn't have been able to spell it. While other branch members stocked their humour arsenals with the comic equivalents of the multi-warhead missile, Colin was still struggling to master the Stone Age club of the mother-in-law joke.

In fact, he was completely oblivious of the seriousness of his situation. As far as he was concerned, he'd had this idea of holding a huge international diving exhibition in the sleepy Dorset village of Sturminster (population 2325) and nobody came. Oh, well, he'd reflected philosophically in the snug of The Cat & Hacksaw, that was Life. It was just the way Things sometimes Went. It wasn't really anybody's fault. Not as such.

Anyway, looking on the bright side, a lot of very famous names in the diving world had turned up. And they'd given him tremendous amounts of money to put up their stands in the old Civil Defence Drill Hall on Bath Street.

Colin hadn't spent all of it, of course.

Chairman: "Exactly how much did you spend, Mister Mouldey?"

Colin: "Er, now there you've got me, sir. I did write it down, special like, but blow me if I 'aven't lost the bit o' paper. I remember there was the RIB an' the engine. Engines, I should say. An' the compressor. And... and..."

Voice: "And the Mexican liveaboard trip."

Colin: "Oy aye! Thanks, Frank. That would account for it, then. I'd forgot about Mexico. Funny 'ow the mind plays tricks."

Chairman: "Mister Mouldey. I may be no mathematician, but the items you've enumerated so far, even including a holiday in Mexico, would only seem to account for a tiny fraction of the overall discrepancy. You must have omitted something. I urge you to cast your mind back."

Colin: "Um... er... I know! There was the barbecue."

Voice: "And the boat trailer."

The Inquiry was rapidly descending into a nightmare version of *The Generation Game.*

Colin: "Yeah, that's it! The trailer. Ta, Norman."

Voice Two: "An' the global video navigator."

Voice Three: "And the armoured Forward Command Vehicle we got from the Israelis."

Colin: "The FCV, yes!"

Voice Four: "An' the 'orse."

Chairman: "Stop! Stop! I won't have this inquiry turned into a bear garden."

Colin: "No, sir, it were an 'orse. Hannibal. Alf's right. I'd forgot about Hannibal."

Chairman (sighing wearily): "Forgive my ignorance, Mister Mouldey, I am merely a layman in diving terms, appointed by the British Sub-Aqua Club to conduct this inquiry as an independent and disinterested Chair.

"The significance of boats to a diving club, and of associated nautical paraphernalia, I can readily comprehend. Even that of a barbecue and a specialised motor vehicle. But I fear I shall need enlightenment as to the place in your organisation's inventory that

might be occupied by an 'orse."

Colin: "Yeah, I see your point, Mr Chair. It was all a bit of an embarrassin' error, as it 'appens. Y'see, this feller called me up from Newcastle, 'e was – an' asked if we wanted to buy the 'war horse'. Well, we'd just come back from a trip an' we'd been divin' on the *War Horse* an' we'd always talked about the idea of actually ownin' a wreck an'… an'… well, it seemed like a good idea at the time."

Chairman (tetchily): "I don't understand why this should have necessitated your purchasing – and I quote here from the vet's report – 'a cankered, 18-year-old ex-dray horse with arthritis, windgalls, equine lymphangitis, mud fever and chronic ear mites'.

"In short, Mister Mouldey, a spavin, sway-backed nag, for whom the municipal glue factory would have offered a merciful release."

Colin: "It was 'is Geordie accent, your Chairship. He wasn't sayin' 'war horse' at all. He was sayin' 'our horse'."

Chairman: "So what did you say?"

Colin: "I said, 'Why, that's what I call a bloody wreck, mate!'"

Chairman: "And what did he say?"

Colin: "He said something like 'You're not bloody wrong there, mate!'"

Chairman: "Mister Mouldey. All this makes perfect sense to me now. But one aspect of your story still puzzles me. Why did this... Geordie gentleman... call you in the first place? You're not an equestrian, are you?"

Colin: "No, your Lud. They wouldn't 'ave me, on account of I wouldn't wear the apron. No, I 'spect it was just a wrong number, an' as luck would 'ave it, he found 'imself talkin' to a kindred spirit."

Chairman: "Yes, Mister Mouldey, I'm sure that's exactly how the mix-up occurred. But, in a sense, it's all entirely academic. For according to my calculations, Sturminster Parva has acquired a debt in excess of £130,000. A debt, I may add, which is accumulating interest at a compounded annual rate of 264.5 per cent, thanks to some highly questionable borrowing."

Colin: "Now 'old fast there, your Honourableness! That's not fair! Barracuda Ned has been a good friend to this branch since..."

At this point, the proceedings were violently interrupted by Mrs Rene Mouldey, who burst into the lounge of The Smiling Accountant, triumphantly waving a slip of paper.

"Col!" she cried. "Col, he done it! 'Annibal! He come in three 'undred 'an fifty to one in the St Abb's!"

And our Treasurer smiled. "That's just the way things go, sometimes. I mean, that's Life. Innit?"

Last call for
Anthrax Point

"COME ON, George, prise those buggers out of the bar, or we'll be 'ere all night. Let's convene the meeting."

And thus, in the time-honoured tradition of Sturminster Parva Branch, commenced our first committee meeting of the new season.

"Right. First off – Financial Report and Accounts. Terence, are things looking up since Colin Mouldey's... er... departure?"

"Thanks, Big Norman. Well, it's been a funny old year. Things were looking a bit bleak in January, when they repossessed the van.

"As you all know, we managed to scrape by without selling the compressor to the Iraqis. But nobody likes to live hand-to-mouth. It's bad for the nerves. I mean, supposing Hannibal hadn't come in at 350 to 1 at Cheltenham; where would we be now, I ask you?

"So this year, we're going to take some preventive measures. For a start, we're going to conduct a Personal Means Audit of every Branch member. Those who slot into Band A – that is, with total assets in excess of £100,000 – will be required to bequeath to the branch a sum equalling no less than 20 per cent of their estates, this being calculated after death duties.

"Obviously, the Committee sees this as a long-term palliative only – except in your case, George! Hey, only kidding mate; 83's no age these days, is it?

"So those with assets of between £50,000 and £99,000 – that's Band B – shall be expected to make the branch an interest-free loan equal to one month's income, gross. Payment should be made in the form of a money order or equivalent instrument, made out to Terrinorm Enterprises (Grand Cayman) Ltd.

"Those unfortunate members who, thanks to the ravages of the national recession, find themselves caught in the so-called 'negative equity trap' will be excused with appropriate donations of share certificates, negotiable bonds, cutlery, etc."

"Thank you, Terence. I know the membership will join me in expressing appreciation for your unstinting efforts on behalf of the branch during these difficult times. Remember all, that's Terrinorm – one word.

"Now, on to more positive things. Next season's diving! Without further ado, I'll call upon our Diving Officer to run the options by us. Dave?"

"Ta, Norm. Yes, well. Me an' the Sub-Committee thought we'd 'ave a break from tradition. In the past, as you all know, we've kicked off the season every year with an Easter splash at Bovvy.

"So this year, cash bein' a bit tight an' all, we've booked the second Monday in June at Bletchley Brick Ponds. Always a great day's divin', is the Brick Ponds, an' we're expecting a big turn-out. So – cheques and postal orders, please, for £85 per head, made payable to Davinorm (Grand Cayman) Ltd."

"Yes, sorry Dave, that's Davinorm. One word."

"Thanks, Norman. Now you may be wonderin' why we're startin' so late this year. It's on account of the forthcomin' Chairman's Reconnaissance Expedition, which'll mean that certain key officers of the branch will be away in the Cayman Islands on branch business from the middle of March to the end of May.

"Frankly, if you want my opinion, it's more than a nuisance; it's a bloody disgrace. Nobody's more narked than I am that the entire branch have to sit on their backsides while three senior committee members live it up in the Caribbean, stayin' in five-star hotels on full expenses.

"I can only say – and I know I speak for Norman and Terry, too – that we'll be back just as soon as we can blag an upgrade to Business Class.

"Now I think you'll concede that I've always striven to reflect the diverse interests of the membership in the selection o' dive sites. And so it's with some pride that I announce our first expedition, arranged specifically with the conservationist element in mind.

"As you know, there's been a lot o' controversy surroundin' the sitin' of a third live sewage outfall in the Tees estuary, between the Urea Plant at Billingham and the Polytetrafluorethelene

Dibinitrobenzoate Cracking Facility at Cargo Fleet.

"Well, now's your chance to do something about it, instead of sittin' around in the bar of the Cat & Hacksaw, night after bleedin' night, like a bunch of moanin' minnies, curin' all the world's ills with a pint in yer 'and. No offence meant.

"Because on August Bank Holiday, instead of the usual seal dive in the Farnes, we'll be dropping into the estuary just off Anthrax Point – you know, where they dumped the cattle during the last war – and drifting down on the outfall with special measurin' equipment supplied by Greenpeace.

"Sorry, I didn't catch that. Do you need a special suit? Quick answer: I won't, you might. I'll 'ave to refer you to Doctor Bill Crombie on that one, pal. He'll be leadin' the dive, on account of me bein' away for the whole of August, testin' the new TechnoPro fins in Papua New Guinea.

"Personally, I'm gutted that I won't be able to join you for this 'istoric and scientifically crucial expedition. It is, of course, vitally important that the membership wholeheartedly supports Dr Crombie – and we on the committee will take a pretty dim view, I can tell you, of anyone who's able to join the dive but doesn't.

"Frankly, any such person would be effectively kissin' goodbye to any chance of servin' the branch as an officer in the future.

"But then, if one was out of the country at the time, I'd say this would constitute an acceptable reason for absence.

"And as it 'appens, I seem to recall that TechnoPro are still lookin' for fin testers for their Papua New Guinea trip. Anyone interested should see me after the meetin' with a valid medical certificate an' a cheque for £2450.67 made out to TechnoDave (Grand Cayman) Ltd.

"That's TechnoDave. One word."

Winter blues at the Cat & Hacksaw

WINTER is a grisly time for us aquanauts. A dropped stitch in life's rich tapestry. A dark and joyless limbo zone, where the hours drag painfully by, slower even than our brand new £10,000 RIB after Barney Melsom topped up the fuel tank with dandelion and burdock.

Between November and April, I seldom leave my bed. I lie in a state of semi-coma, haunted by the terrifying denizens of nightmare.

Last night, I dreamed I left the Heinke Trophy on the bus from Stoney Cove to Truk Lagoon. I was tried by a jury of wreck divers from Cardiff Branch, and sentenced to listen to Mike Todd's dive computer lecture for eternity. I started from my sleep, sweat-drenched and quaking with terror.

It was club night. With a tremendous effort of will, I dragged myself out of the house and down to the Cat & Hacksaw. There, at least, I could mingle with my fellow divers, perhaps lay plans for the next season, and recall the highlights and triumphs of the last day.

It was a sorry scene that awaited me. A handful of pale men in macs, so diminished by the drab uniform of the English Winter Brigade that I hardly recognised them. Surely, that couldn't be Arthur "Madman" Wilkins, who got himself arrested last August at Seahouses for trying to barbecue the harbourmaster? He looks so sad and small, now, hunched over a half of flat shandy, cleaning his spectacles with the bar coaster.

And isn't that… no, it can't be… Betty-Ann Polanski, who ate Colin's gloves for a bet in the Bovisand bar? The bronzed, Amazon goddess who beat all-comers in the outboard tossing competition at our famous Apache Evening, after six mugs of mulled absinthe?

Polanski was simply not constructed for any garment besides her scarlet lurex and neoprene kimono, slashed to the waist, that afforded such tantalising glimpses of the jewel-encrusted Abyssinian diving stiletto she kept strapped to her thigh.The tweed skirt and wellies did nothing for her at all.

I ordered my customary quart of Beaston's Old Daftbugger and tried to make conversation.

"How was the Karaoke Night?" I enquired of the Social Secretary.

"Wash out. Three people turned up. Nigel Fishwick had to sing the whole of Mozart's Requiem to fill the time."

I paused for a moment, then soldiered on. "Dennis!" I cried. "Me old buddy! Done any diving recently?"

"Nah." He wouldn't meet my eyes. "Not cold enough. I'll dive when you can skate on Gildenburgh."

Hah! Did I detect a faint spark of the old spirit? "Good boy! And I'll come with you! We'll take Colin, too!"

"Colin isn't diving with us anymore," he replied flatly. "He went to see Peter Wilmshurst for his regular medical. Wilmshurst pronounced him fit, then asked him to participate in this experiment he was running. He agreed and, well, it turns out he's HIB positive."

I was dumbfounded. "What? You mean… Oh, God, I'm sorry, I never… HIV."

"No, no. HIB – Hole In The Brain. Ninety-five per cent of the population has one, apparently. It's a birth defect."

"How can you tell?"

"It's not always obvious. You might, say, exhibit a tendency to enjoy *Blind Date*. And there's a slight but measurable propensity to vote Conservative. But it only *really* comes to light when you dive."

"Go on. How does it manifest itself?"

"Well, in Colin's case, he accepted an invitation to dive with Whitby Branch. That was the first sign. Nobody said anything, of course. I mean, you don't, do you?"

"And then what?"

"He put himself forward for Diving Officer, took up octopush and bought two books by Kendall McDonald."

"Surely not? That's too horrible."

"It was just the start."

"What do you mean? Surely he didn't…"

"He did. He joined PADI."

I sat down heavily. "I don't believe it."

"It's true. He told me last January. We were driving back to Poole in the RIB in a Force 6 and it was`snowing and the light was going and we were running low on fuel and the radio was on the blink and he just came out with it. "Sod this, Dennis," he said, "I fancy diving in me kegs and me T-shirt in warm, clear Caribbean water, surrounded by clouds of breathtakin'ly gorgeous reef fish, then popping up for a quick pina colada with a couple of scantily clad nymphettes on the bridge of a gleamin' white trimaran with a satellite navigator and a CD player in the saloon."

"Well, stick me in the pot and take me down to 90m. Is there any… hope?"

"I'm afraid it's too late. Before I could stop him, he'd done the cross-over course. Now he's in the British Virgin Islands, with only three or four air hostesses for company. Tragic."

"Can't anything be done for him?"

"Believe me, we've tried. I wrote and invited him to the branch weekend in Skegness, but he didn't even reply. I'm afraid he's beyond help."

"It's such a waste," he added. "I mean, look what he's missing."

I glanced around the snug. There was old Guppy Sinclair, dozing in front of the coal-effect fire, his pint slowly spilling down his Terylene tie.

Gladys Saunders was sitting in her usual corner with a milk stout, stuffing old drysuits with beach tar to make draught excluders for the Branch car boot sale.

Derek and Maisie Pigeon were busy loading the carousel for the main event of the evening – a slide show entitled *Brick Pits of The East Midlands: A Secret World Of Pleasure.*

A couple of excited novices were discussing the body-shell of the 1955 Ford Prefect they'd found during a night dive in the Manchester Ship Canal.

Hailstones rattled against the window.

My heart went out to Colin. "That poor man," I murmured. "That poor, poor man."

My packet of porky scratchings lay unopened on the table.

All in the name of fun

IT WAS a September evening at the Cat & Hacksaw, spiritual home of the branch. The entertainments sub-committee was wrapping up its quarterly meeting in the lounge bar.

Meanwhile, in the snug, the Ancient Diver ruminated quietly in the corner (we'd long since given up trying to cure him of it. You can't teach an old sea dog new tricks).

He peered into the spluttering fire (see what I mean?) and then he cleared his throat with a sound like a ton of slush sliding off an old tin roof. He drew on his pipe. He drew on the walls, too, and on the tables, and on the accumulated experience of a lifetime's diving. On one occasion, he drew on his savings and was arrested for defacing the currency of the realm.

He raised his shaggy head, and his hoary old locks gleamed in the firelight. It was the signal that he was About To Speak – and there appeared about him magically a circle of respectful listeners.

For a long moment he contemplated a genie of pungent smoke from his briar as it curled towards the ceiling. And then, in a barnacle-encrusted voice from the floor of a bottomless sea, he said: "Entertainments committee? Yer all a bunch of bloody nancies.

"In my day, we made our own entertainment. We didn't have no committee tellin' us what were entertainin' and what weren't. Why, I remember the Summer Splash of '52. We were doing a 200ft night dive on the wreck of the *Death Watch Beetle*, and Big Norman filled one of the bottles with nitrous oxide, then shuffled them around so nobody knew which one it was.

"How we laughed! Well, Ollie Rangecroft laughed, anyroad – 'cos it was 'im who got the laughin' gas. Laughed till he cried, did Ollie, down at 200ft in the dark. That's what I call entertainment."

"What happened to Mister Rangecroft?" piped up a wide-eyed novice.

The Ancient Diver frowned. "Can't rightly recall. I 'spect he was alright. Maybe he wasn't. Maybe that was somebody else…"

During the old man's tale, the Social Secretary had become restless, then visibly uncomfortable, then downright indignant.

"It all sounds highly irresponsible to me," he exclaimed. "Very dangerous, in fact."

"You can't make an omelette without breakin' eggs," pronounced the Ancient Diver darkly.

The Soc Sec continued: "This is 1998 and I'm sure that our members were quite sufficiently entertained by our recent Norwegian Evening." He swivelled in his seat and elected one of the audience at random. "What did *you* think of our Norwegian Evening, Dave?"

Now it was Dave's turn to look uncomfortable. "Well, er… I thought it was… um… well… crap. Actually."

There was the sort of silence you get after a terrorist bomb, thick and dusty. "Crap? Crap?" repeated the Soc Sec slowly. "I take it you've forgotten Derek and Maisie's slides of Trondheim? I assume that Inga's demonstration of the Norske lemming dance has somehow slipped your memory?"

Dave just stared at his big shoes.

The Soc Sec rose. "Right! Fine! I think I'm beginning to understand. Come on then, let's get it all out in the open! Anybody else want to criticise the – *my* – entertainments programme? Don't be shy, now – speak up!"

"Aye, me!"

The Soc Sec gave a bitter little laugh. "Et tu, Colin? All right. What was it that didn't live up to your ever-so-elevated expectations?"

"The Scrabble Challenge."

"Hah! Did you hear that, everybody? Colin found the Scrabble Challenge disappointing. Nothing whatsoever to do with the fact that he was knocked out in the very first round by Ho Tse Chang, the only non-English speaking member of the branch! Anybody else?"

"Yeah!" This time it was Bomber Snudden, Expeditions Officer, ex-2 Para, Tai Kwando Champion of the Medway Towns. "Yeah. I'd just like to ask what exac'ly is the relevance to a divin' club of a three-hour lecture on fretwork?"

"Hear, hear!" called first one, then a growing number of the assembled crowd.

"Wait! Quiet! If I might be allowed to answer Bomber's question? The relevance, Bomber, is simply this: that the mastery of such a demanding and precise craft as creative fretwork represents an important example to the diver – an object lesson in the value of patience, of attention to detail, of pride in achievement, that we would all do well to heed."

"Nothin' whatsoever to do with the fact, then," pursued Bomber, "that the fretwork lecturer just happened to be the Social Secretary's brother-in-law?"

(Laughter from the Rough Element.)

The Soc Sec flushed. "I'm saddened that you should entertain so low an opinion of me, Bomber. I thought we were friends. I can only say that my sole aim in my capacity as Social Secretary has been to provide a varied programme of instructive and improving *divertissements* for the members of the branch it has been my privilege to serve."

"Then why did you put a block on the Cabinet Ministers and Actresses Party, then?" called the Training Officer. "That would've been instructive."

(Hoots of derisive laughter from the entire company.)

And what happened to the Boat People Raft Race? Ho Tse Chang spent bloody weeks on that sampan, and you cancelled it without a vote! You're a bloody cultural dictator, that's what you are."

(Wild cheering.)

"The Boat People event was cancelled because certain senior members of the Branch felt it was in poor taste."

"Aye, like the Dwarf Throwin'!"

"And the Pig Rodeo!"

The Soc Sec struggled to swim against the flood tide of revolution. "Now you can't blame the Pig Rodeo cancellation on me. That was the RSPCA."

"Resign! Resign!"

It was then that the Ancient Diver stepped in. He banged his pewter mug on the table and rose unsteadily to his feet. "That's meer like it, lads. It's aboot time we 'ad a bit o' fun round 'ere. I say we kick off the new season like in the old days with a Munitions Party. Everyone 'as to bring along summat suspicious from the Lulworth area, and we chuck it on t'barbecue. First one to run for cover's a nancy."

(Awkward silence.)

It was the Soc Sec who eventually spoke up, with all the self-assurance of a newly restored dictator. "Any takers for a Cluedo Evening?"

Divers who can, and divers who can't

"HERE'S A TIP," confided the Equipment Officer, in the snug of the Cat & Hacksaw.

"Bung a bit of calcium carbide on a slice of bread and feed it to the gulls."

And he winked at me lasciviously.

I don't know about you, but I hate our Equipment Officer. He's living proof of the adage, "a little knowledge is a dangerous thing". He's a lethal human cocktail – one part Einstein, ten parts Oliver Reed. He's the logical consequence of Leonardo da Vinci being voted Social Secretary of Millwall Supporters Club.

"OK," I surrender wearily. "What happens?"

He grins. "They explode."

"What?"

"See, calcium carbide plus water equals huge volumes of acetylene gas. Well, yer seagull's got a non-return value in 'is throat to stop the fish poppin' out. So, bam! Seagull explodes. QE bleedin' D! Ready for another pint?"

"Not really, no. Thanks…"

I mean, how does someone get to know that kind of thing? Do you attend secret candle-lit Equipment Officers' suppers in disused subterranean chalk workings, where you swap monstrous pseudo-scientific experiments over jugs of industrial grade lager?

Or is there a book? *The Equipment Officer's Guide To Crude And Brutal Demonstrations Of Physical Principles? Nuclear Fission For Vizigoths?*

The really irritating thing is, though, he really does know what he's doing. You can't write him off as a sort of Raging Bull with a monkey wrench. He only has to glance at something to know what's wrong with it.

"What's the prob, Chief?"

"Well, every time I breathe in, my lungs fill with water, paralysing me with panic so that I begin to drown."

"Have you tried putting the regulator in yer mouth? You 'ave? Then it's the worm gear in the A-stage inlet valve lower manifold compensator assembly."

"Is that serious?"

"Put it this way – send it back to Sub-World Aquanautica Interglobal and it'll take 'em six months and cost you fifty quid.

"On the other 'and, give it me now and I'll fix it on the spot for the price of an 'air grip, two ring-pulls and a whatchamacallit."

"What, er, kind of whatchamacallit?"

"You know, a thingumybob. An owsyerfather? Somethin' for the weekend, sir?"

"Mm? Oh, no thanks, we're going away, actually, to visit the wife's parents and…"

"Oh, lawks! A *condom*, mate!"

"Ah. Yes. Well, how much does a… one of those… cost? Actually?

"Blimey, pal, you must lead an exciting life! They don't come in ones, not since the days Woodbines did. But don't worry, I've got 'undreds. Mate of mine's on the vans, know what I mean?"

I didn't, but I nodded sagely, and handed him the DV. Ten minutes later, it was back in my dive bag, good as new. For Storm (that's his name – it's tattooed across his upper arm, just above the striking panel in green and purple that reads: "Sleep with me and dive for free") is a kind of genius.

Which brings me to the real point of this story – namely, that to be a Proper Diver, you have to be a *Can*.

The diving world is divided not into *Haves* and *Have-Nots*, but into *Cans* and *Can'ts*.

If the outboard should make a strange, knocking noise while the boat drags its anchor in a Force 7 off Cape Wrath, the Can will cheerfully dismantle it down to the last spring washer; then reassemble it, the knock identified and eliminated, before his divers surface.

The Can't, on the other hand, will immediately broadcast a Mayday signal on the boat radio. If help does not arrive within 20 seconds, he will assume the radio is malfunctioning.

In this situation, the Can will calmly check the battery terminal, adjust the gain, perhaps clean the aerial connection. Whereas the Can't will throw the set overboard.

And there you have it. One views machines as the mindless servants of mankind, perhaps complex, but never complicated – the epitomy of common sense, cast in steel and aluminium.

The other recognises that everything mechanical is invested with a demoniacal will of its own, and is joining together with other bits of machinery and electronic jumble in a fiendish conspiracy to get its own back on us humans.

Incidentally, the Can't should not be confused with the *Won't*. The Won't is a Can who Could, and conceivably Would if offered sufficient material inducement. However, on branch dives, the Won't prefers to masquerade as a Can't, thus avoiding all danger of physical or mental effort.

I am the Supreme Chief Executive and Life President of the Can'ts.

In order to go diving, I require the support of a vast army of Cans. Experts to tell me I've put my suit on back to front. That my stab jacket is inside out. That I'm rinsing my DV in two-stroke.

People to carry my spare O-ring, to hand me my weightbelt after my tenth attempt to descend without it, to understand my decompression tables for me.

If divers were countries, our Equipment Officer would be Germany. I would be Haiti.

What we have here, of course, is a perfect microcosm of man's essential schizophrenia. For in each of us there is an engineer and a poet. The engineer invented the wheel – the poet dreamed the Ferrari.

Certainly, the poet needs the engineer. Who wants a Ferrari without wheels? But then again, what's the point of being able to fix the radio if you've got nothing to say?

In fact, what's the point of diving at all, if you reduce it to a clinical demonstration of the Gas Laws?

There has to be a balance. And this is best expressed by Blackford's Law, namely: in any given diving club, there must exist one silly Can't for every ten, sensible Cans. In my branch, I'm happy to say, I am that silly Can't.

Buddying up with the Mister Pastry of the diving world

THERE IS nothing so satisfying as watching a new diver's progress. From awkward novice, hesitant and uncertain, beset with fears and doubts, to master of the sport – strong, self-assured, armed with new skills and new confidence.

We briny old seadogs watch indulgently those first, tentative steps in the pool. With silent pride we are witness to the Great Day – that first open-water dive, in 9m of opaque industrial waste off the South Coast.

We observe the exams, the wrestling with the Tables, the incessant intoning of the Gas Laws, like some medieval, monastic catechism.

And lo! Before long, they emerge from the chrysalis of the lecture room as competent, qualified divers.

However, just occasionally, the butterfly turns out to be a dung beetle. A clumsy, bumbling disaster.

You know exactly who I mean. The one who dusted his drysuit with itching powder instead of talc.

The one who mixed the two-stroke in the inverse proportions.

The one who failed to raise the Swanage coastguard on the club radio, but succeeded in ruining a phone-in on Radio Free Angola.

For some reason, never satisfactorily explained, nearly all such inepts are called Colin.

In fact, in an attempt to contain the problem, the BSAC is to launch a special, all-Colin branch. There is some debate as to where Colin Branch should be situated. Personally, I favour Krakatoa, although there's a strong lobby for Chernobyl.

You may recall that my own branch has a Colin. Colin, the

Directionally Dyslexic. Despite his disability, by the immutable law of Sod, he invariably ends up at the helm on any expedition demanding the skills and instincts of the born navigator.

Whenever you hear Colin's name mentioned (which is about as often as you hear the Lord's Prayer recited backwards), there invariably springs to mind the famous Farnes trip.

We set off from Seahouses in conditions of flat calm – rare on that stretch of coast – and perfect visibility. The sky was a deep and radiant azure.

The usual "shag or cormorant?" debate ensued, I recall, and we gaily slashed at each other's low-pressure hoses with our branch-issue Toledo steel machetes.

The Farnes seemed but a stone's throw away.

In retrospect, the authorities at Trondheim could have been a bit more sympathetic. After all, Briton and Norwegian are bound together by a Viking bloodline, deeper, surely, than the mere red tape of petty bureaucracy.

But, as the Consul pointed out when he visited us before the trial, piracy is still a serious offence. Several delegates to the Pan-Scandinavian Congress of Churches had to be revived with smelling salts and winched off their chartered launch by helicopter, following the regrettable business with the flare and the Bishop's dachshunds.

Only one thing is worse than Colin the Driver, and that is Colin the Diver. When he announces to the Marshal his intention to dive, the word flies around the branch like a grass fire.

Experienced divers unaccountably develop debilitating migraines. Cries of "Oh damn, I've broken a wrist seal" and "Look, I hate to be a party pooper, but the old knee business is giving me gip" reverberate about the site.

It's usually some raw recruit, fresh-faced and pitifully naive, who pipes up, "Colin's a Dive Leader. Surely I could dive with him?" Muffled sniggers come from behind the van.

Don't misunderstand me. Colin has been diving for years, and his kit is first rate. It's just that Colin and his kit rarely dive together. Either his fins and mask go overboard while he remains in the boat, or else he slips gracefully into the embracing bosom of the ocean while his weightbelt relaxes in the boot of his car.

In the rare event of his submerging with all his equipment,

those up-side will stake their beer money on how long it will take him to bob up to the surface, bound tightly in the buoy-line like Tutankhamun's mummy.

Give him a line and a skeg to foul it with, and Colin becomes a sort of reverse Houdini – a highly accomplished *entangologist.*

Yet he's been a loyal branch member for 20 years. What makes him stick at it?

I suppose it could be the social side of things – but then, he hasn't been invited to a "do" since he marinated the roasting pig in two-stroke "to get it going".

Nor does he get the chance to handle the boats much these days. Not since he offered to moor the RIB for the night, and tied it to the head of the DO of Whitby Branch. Fortunately, one of the frigates picked them up at dawn, 30 miles west of the Scillies.

Colins are nothing if not keen. Ours will put his name down for everything. He volunteered three times for the Bovisand explosives course, but he never got to take it. As soon as the list went up, everybody else dropped out. Sheer bad luck.

The last time, he even offered to pay the whole course fee himself, and do the whole thing solo. But the instructor came down with suspected bubonic and spent the next three months in an isolation hospital. Just in case.

And as a matter of historical interest, it was thanks to Colin that the 30m Assisted Ascent was dropped from the old Second Class syllabus. Not only did he assist the ascent of his buddy, but also of the two branch instructors who were supervising the test. Then he attempted the Assisted Descent of a brace of perch fishermen who, until then, had been quietly contemplating the majesty of the sunset over Bletchley Brick Ponds.

From time to time, Colinism poses a serious political problem at committee level. A Colin will enthusiastically put himself forward for every office in the branch, and there's always someone with enough mischief, malice or plain cloth-headedness to second him.

So how do you tell the Mister Pastry of the diving world that he doesn't possess in sufficient abundance the special qualities that characterise the ideal Chairman?

Simple. Do what we did.

Make him Diving Officer.

A history lesson down at the local

THE ANCIENT DIVER sat in the pub. Rather, the pub seemed to sit around the Ancient Diver, as if one day, long ago, in a time before pubs, he had appointed a very special spot in the middle of a field and had sat down heavily and exactly and irrevocably upon it.

And while the centuries swung clamorously by, not a ripple had marred the perfect calm of his complacency.

Finally, in 1937, Barsted's Brewery built the Cat & Hacksaw in front of him and behind, to the left and the right, the above and below. And there he sits to this day, a 16-inch naval shell case of Old Badger Breath clasped in a paw like the bucket on a JCB.

The other paw makes the long, slow ascent to his mouth, where it dabs beery foam from a wire-wool beard.

He speaks. His voice is deep and deliberate, like the beat of a ship's engines. It invests his words with the irresistible momentum of a dreadnought.

"'Course, in my day, you didn't have all the fancy kit. Not when I started divin'."

These words were addressed to nobody and to everybody. The crowd at The Cat & Hacksaw has heard them many times before, until they have assumed a sort of liturgical quality – like the "Kyrie" in a high German mass, or the "Good Morning!" at the start of Alistair Cooke's *Letter From America*.

The regulars at the Cat, divers all, know they're going to hear the Equipment Is For Pansies monologue, and they are resigned and yet contented. The Ancient Diver would speak, and this was how things should always be, had always been.

"There was a couple down on Swanage pier last weekend, and

what did they look like? I ask yer. Like a couple of bloody go-go dancers, that's what. Pink and sky-blue wetsuits – luminous, with it. I told 'em, they'd have gone down a treat at The Smirking Steward, over by the ferry terminal. They'd have turned a head or two in the snug down there, take my word."

"In my day, the pioneerin' days, we used to make our own suits. And they weren't bloody pink, neither.

"An old plastic mac, a pair of the wife's nylons and a rubber band, that's all we needed. And a pea colander, two dustbin lids, the lead off a church roof, a sheepskin rug, a brace of 'ot water bottles, a theodolite, 20ft of good hemp rope an' a pound of tripe. That's all.

"It might've been simple, but it worked. And what did it cost? Not a penny over six hundred quid."

He drained his shell case and banged it down on the table so hard that the portrait of Kendall McDonald crashed to the floor from its place above the fireplace.

The Ancient Diver continued, oblivious. "These two 'ad more pipes and tubes stickin' out of them than the Brighouse & Rastrick Brass Band.

"One of 'em – the girl or the feller, you couldn't tell which was what for blinkin' paraphernalia – one of 'em 'ad a computer strapped on its arm. A *computer!* Said it told 'em when to come up.

"We never 'ad no computers. Didn't need 'em. You knew when it was time to come up when the blood came out yer nose, and you 'eard the orchestra.

"If they were playin' "Oh, What A Beautiful Morning" from *Oklahoma!,* you knew you could stop down a bit longer. It was when they did "Abide With Me", you had to go for the surface like a rat up a flue. Never failed."

The Ancient Diver shifted the pommel of his wooden leg in its dish of linseed oil. The circumstances surrounding his amputation were shrouded in speculation. Some say he cut off his own leg to avoid carrying an outboard up Chesil Beach.

Asked why he had opted for a wooden replacement when modern artificial limb design favoured strong, light alloys, he would permit himself a sly smile: "What? Dive with Whitby Branch, wearin' a non-ferrous leg? I might be simple, but I'm not daft. Before you could say, 'pass me the lump 'ammer' there'd be bits of me on every mantlepiece from here to Robin Hood's Bay."

"An' all this nonsense about boats. Rigid 'ulls and softboats and 'ardboats. When we wanted to dive on a wreck, we just used to pick a trawler from t'arbour, drive her out into deep water, pull the plug and go down with the ship. Saved a lot o' muckin' about. 'Course, you 'ad to swim 'ome."

A young novice dared to point out that such a practice might, in some small way, have contributed to the traditional suspicion of divers felt by the fishing community.

"Nay, lass. We got on famously. It were give an' take. We'd sink their boats and slash their nets and pinch their lobbies and wink at their wives, and they'd try to shoot us in the water with 'igh powered 'unting rifles. It was a bit of a game, that's all. No 'ard feelings, or owt.

"In fact, I recall the time the fisherfolk filled Old Tom's bottle with acetylene gas when he wasn't lookin'. How we laughed. He went up like the *R101*. It was on a night dive, too, and they say you could see the flames from Middlesbrough. But there wasn't any harm in it. Just a bit of high jinks.

"But things have changed. There isn't the same feelin' of brotherhood among men as what there was in my day."

And with a great grunting and groaning, the Ancient Diver pulled himself to his feet. "I'll be off then. I'm whittlin' a new demand valve out of a mahogany dresser and the light's goin'. You can't be too careful, not with the price of candles what it is."

And as he heaved his huge bulk through the door of the Cat & Hacksaw and into the evening, we could still hear him, addressing the twilight and the first glimmering stars and the timeless rolling sea: "'Course, in my day, we didn't need candles…"

Vote Desirée!

THE MARVELLOUS thing about diving is the complete absence of politics.

I hate politics. I work for an advertising agency. You know when it's a good day, because you only get stabbed in the front.

Not so with diving. When I go along to the diving club, I put all that machiavellian manoeuvring behind me.

The BSAC, after all, is an association of amateurs, in the best sense of the word – committed individuals, drawn together by a shared passion for the sport, and a selfless desire to promote conservation, safety and the advancement of knowledge among our members.

There simply isn't room in our excellent organisation for personal ambition. Why, it occurred to me only the other day at our Branch AGM that the politicians have a lot to learn from us divers when it comes to good, old-fashioned statesmanship and uncomplaining self-sacrifice.

My thoughts were interrupted by Julian, last year's Treasurer. In fact, he couldn't have shocked me more if he'd tossed me a live hand-grenade. "Can I get you a pint?" he said.

Now, as anyone who knows him even a little will testify, the juxtaposition of Julian and the offer of a drink is positively surreal. About as likely as a hand of strip poker with Mother Teresa.

I was almost too thunderstruck to accept, but not quite.

We stood at the bar and exchanged pleasantries.

Then he said: "Um, er, looks as if it could be quite a close-run thing for Diving Officer."

"Could be," I agreed, "but I rather think Ken'll get it. He's a good bloke. Solid."

Julian looked faintly uncomfortable, shifted his weight to the other foot. "Oh, solid, certainly. As a rock."

"And he's put in the hours," I pursued. He's worked for it."

"Absolutely," Julian conceded. "No doubt about that. It's just…"

"Just what?"

"Oh, nothing."

"What?"

"No, really, it's nothing at all. He's solid, like you say."

My curiosity was aroused, now.

"Come on, Julian, what are you trying to say? What's wrong with the idea of Ken as DO?"

"Well, it's just that… you don't think he might be a little too solid? A bit… uninspiring, perhaps?"

"What… unadventurous, you mean?"

"Perhaps, a little. Don't you think? I mean, probably not the person to push back the frontiers of the sport – to lead the branch into uncharted waters, to boldly go, et cetera, et cetera?"

"Well, now that you mention it, I suppose he is rather safe. But then, that's what a DO's got to be, isn't it? Safe?"

"Ah yes, Andrew," and he fixed me with a meaningful look, "But there's safe and there's safe. See what I mean?"

I could honestly say, "No."

"Well, let me put it another way. There's Safe-Responsible; Safe-Sensible; Safe-I've-Carefully-Assessed-The-Conditions-And-In-My-Capacity-As-Elected-Diving-Officer-Of-The-Branch-I-Deem-The-Sea-Conditions-Too-Rough-For-Diving. And then there's Safe-Bloody-Downright-Let's-All-Nod-Off-BORING!"

"So – let's get this right – you're saying Ken's a bit… boring?"

"A bit? A BIT? He makes John Major look like Oliver Reed. He's about as stimulating as a copy of the 1972 Macclesfield Telephone Directory with the last page missing. He's about as gripping as a production of Ibsen's *Ghosts* by the Brightlingsea Amateur Dramatic Association. When he speaks, birds fall out of the trees in a state of deep coma. When he shows his slides of his last-but-one diving weekend in Scarborough, they bore a hole in the wall."

"True," I allowed.

"Still, he's solid. Another pint?"

"Thanks."

"Not like Roy."

"Sorry?"

"I said, not like Roy. Roy's hardly what you'd call 'solid'. I mean he's a great character and all that, and he's good with the youngsters in the pool. But he's a bit... well..."

"Lightweight?" I ventured.

"Lightweight! That's it! You've really hit the nail on the head. Oh, it's not really a criticism. We can't all be Charlton Heston, can we! But Diving Officer... well, you want a bit of gravitas, don't you? A touch of the Winston Churchill. As opposed to the Basil Brush."

"Come now, that's hardly fair."

"All right, all right. But say you were three miles offshore with a suspected bend case and it's getting dark and the wind's pushing seven and your engine packs up. Who would you choose to be in charge?"

"Well, I suppose, given a straight choice, one or the other, I'd have to go for Winnie."

"Exactly. A half in there, Andrew? Andy?"

"Yes, cheers, Julian. Jules. So where does that leave us? What about Desirée?"

"Woman."

"No? Really? Surely not! You mean, I've spent the last ten years secretly wondering how he got away with wearing lipstick in the pool, and you're telling me he's not a man at all? Good old Des, a woman? Go on, pull the other one."

"I don't think this is an appropriate subject for levity, do you, Andrew? I mean, the standing of the branch is at stake here, not to mention the safety of its members. What I meant was, Desirée's gender cannot be ignored when we consider her suitability for the post of Diving Officer."

"I don't see that."

"Oh, it's not that I've got anything against the Fair Sex. I love every last one of 'em. That goes without saying. It's just the lads, you know."

"The lads."

"Yes, I mean the lads won't be too happy, having a woman as DO. You know what they're like. They're a rough and ready lot."

"Not as rough and ready as Desirée is. If anyone said a word, she'd rip their bloody arms off."

"You're not serious? You're not really going to put Desirée forward?"

"Might."

"Well frankly, Andrew, I'm disappointed by that. It smacks to me of sexual prejudice. Positive discrimination. You're going to vote for her, just because she's a woman."

"You're wrong, Julian," I replied.

"Go on, then, why?"

"It's because you've just bought me two-and-a-half pints of lager."

"So what? What's wrong with that?"

"Well, Desirée bought me three pints last night."

How many crabs can one man eat?

HERE FOLLOW the minutes of 1999 Annual General Meeting of Sturminster Parva Branch of the BSAC, convened on Saturday, 20 December in the Skittle Alley of the Cat & Hacksaw.

The Meeting was called to order at 3.10pm by the outgoing Chairman, Big Norman Bates.

"Right. RIGHT! Let's get this show on the road. Where's the bloody Treasurer?"

Silence.

"Has anyone seen Arthur?"

"I haven't seen him at all today, guvner."

"Well he's supposed to do the financial. Someone give him a call at home, in case he's forgotten. You know what Arthur's like. Meanwhile, Terry, let's do the Diving Officer's bit while we're waiting."

"Yes, thanks Norm. Ahem. Well, we did 14 branch dives this season – some more, er, enthusiastically supported than others.

"Thirty-eight novices turned up for the 70m bounce dive on the ammunition ship in the tidal race off Scapa last January in the blizzard.

"I must say, it hasn't been easy negotiating with the Ministry of Defence. Helicopter time is at a premium these days. But I think we've reached a compromise agreement. Arthur has contacted a pawnbroker in Swanage and we can raise a fair proportion of the money by hocking the RIB. And just possibly the compressor.

"The rest we can scrape together from car boot sales and second mortgages. And I know that Norm has an interesting idea, involving the setting up of a sort of marine escort agency, through which we would rent out the more… personable… branch members as… companions… for lonely, foreign seamen visiting our ports. More about that when Arthur arrives, I expect.

"Where was I? Ah, yes. We had a particularly good turnout for the Sellafield weekend. A propos of which, Mrs Beans has asked me to express Trevor's sincere thanks for all your cards and flowers. When you're stuck in a lead-lined isolation unit under 6m of reinforced concrete, a simple flower says more than words ever can.

"On a less happy note, I feel I do have to mention the Staithes business. Now, we all know that local fishermen can be difficult. They seem to imagine that we divers are motivated by a single, burning ambition – namely to strip them of their livelihoods by plundering their pots.

"But, of course, you and I know that this is only partly true.

"Nevertheless, it was wrong, Dave, very wrong to take the crabs. How many crabs can one man eat, after all? Certainly not 138.

"So you can hardly blame the locals for registering their disapproval. You should just be thankful that Bill had the presence of mind to smother the flames before your drysuit melted. Another two minutes and you'd have been a human jacket potato.

"And whatever you say, Dave, that was no excuse for dynamiting Mr Taylor's septic tank. That was quite unacceptable, and I'm afraid I'm going to have to ask you to return the Hamish Lumsden Trophy, awarded to you by the branch for your 'outstanding contribution to community relations'.

"I only hope you've learned your lesson. High explosives do not sit comfortably in the Caring Nineties, Dave.

"Moving swiftly on, we've got an extremely challenging programme this year. We kick off in early February with the Open Water Test Weekend. Now, I've always maintained that open water should be just that – so this year, we're holding the tests at a point 220 miles north-north-east of Aberdeen.

"As you know, the North Sea is relatively shallow, so I anticipate no special problems with the Roped Search.

"In March, we commence what promises to be the most exciting undertaking in our long and illustrious history.

"In recent years, certain branches of the BSAC have been at the forefront of marine archaeology, with a host of important

discoveries to their credit. Not to be outdone, Sturminster Parva Branch will embark upon a scientific quest of its own. For it is our avowed intention, before the end of 1999, to establish the precise location of Cornwall.

"Now, some of the more senior members may recall that we've attempted to find this elusive site in the past, on two separate occasions.

"The last attempt nearly ended in tragedy when we lost contact with Colin Mouldey and his brave companions for the entire August Bank Holiday weekend. Happily, they were eventually rescued by the RAC outside Carlisle – tired, hungry, but unbowed.

"Of course, technology has marched on since those Spartan times. Nowadays, for instance, we have a van, and poor, faithful old Hannibal has long since dreamed away his last Indian summer at the Horse and Donkey Sanctuary.

"We also have a map – the very latest thing in maps, I'm told –

an unaffordable luxury in Colin's day.

"So anybody who's interested in joining the expedition – and I'm looking here for people with good, basic fitness, who have travelled at least once outside North Dorset – please see me after the meeting. Over to you, Norman."

"Thank you, Terry. And now, is there any word on Arthur?"

"Yes, guv, he's gorn."

"Gorn?"

"Gorn away, 'is landlady says."

"Gone where, for heaven's sake?"

"Ecuador, she says. On a boat. She says he was travellin' light. He left most of his clothes, on account of it's 'ot in Ecuador. All he 'ad was a big bag of money. He told 'er 'is Auntie died and left 'im everythin'."

"For crying out loud! Didn't she suspect something?"

"I dunno, guv. She seemed quite fond of 'im. In fact, she's joinin' 'im in Santa Maria de los Hombres next weekend."

"Well, as Chairman, I have to say I'm stunned. Stunned and deeply disappointed. I mean, I always knew that Arthur favoured a fresh and… creative approach to branch finance. That's why I voted for him. But this…

"I mean, it's bad enough to miss an AGM without so much as a formal note of apology. But what hurts – what really hurts – is that in all the years I've known him, he never told me he had an Auntie."

The branch new kid, the gang, and the van

THIS, REFLECTED Martin Saggers, would undoubtedly be the most exciting day of his life.

The first glimmer of light was disturbing the birds as he crept downstairs. His brand new dive bag waited by the front door, eager as a dog. His brand new aqualung, pristine paintwork glittering behind protective plastic web, seemed charged, not with air, but with pure limitless potential.

He boiled the kettle for his brand new Thermos and removed his sandwiches from the fridge. What fortunate sandwiches they were, to be consumed on such a day.

05.26. In four minutes, the adventure would begin. He checked that his log book was lying perfectly flat at the bottom of his Adidas bag and that his new depth gauge was wrapped up in his spare socks where his comb couldn't scratch it. By the time I put you on, spare socks, I will have been to the bottom of the sea. I will be a Proper Diver.

In two minutes, he would be exchanging manly, jocular greetings with the gang from the Branch. His Branch. His gang. For the first time, he would swing himself up into the cab of the famous van, savour that seductive perfume of rubber, canvas and two-stroke that was the very quintessence of diving…

As it happens, the van didn't turn up until 07.43. There were no jocular greetings, because Tom was in a rage and Matthew was sulking. It seems Matthew had left the keys to the van at the Cat & Hacksaw last night and Ted the landlord could not be roused. The spare set was in the compressor room, but the key to the compressor room wasn't under the stone where it should've been, so Keith must've taken it home with him. The trouble was, Keith lived in

Penge – and in any case, he was probably already on his way to the dive site in Cornwall.

In the end, they'd had to call out the AA who started the van without a key, contrary to AA policy, and advised them to leave the engine running all weekend since they wouldn't be prepared to start it again.

Neither Tom nor Matthew was an AA member, so they'd been obliged to join on the spot (contrary to AA policy). It was while Matthew was looking for his cheque card that he found the key.

Which was why they were two hours late picking up Martin and why Tom was in a rage and Matthew was sulking and why, when they finally arrived at Martin's, there was a noticeable lack of jocularity and manly banter.

"Coffee?" tried Martin, hopefully.

"I don't want your sodding coffee," snarled Tom through gritted teeth. With a fearsome grinding of gears and a sickening lurch, the van embarked upon the long voyage to the English Riviera.

It is better to travel, claims an old Chinese proverb, than to arrive. Clearly, the Chinese had never travelled in the Branch van.

For one thing, the quintessential fragrance of diving was rather more robust and insistent than Martin had anticipated. This was due to an incident some years before, when Big Norman caught a large crayfish and hid it in the back of the van, out of sight of the local fishermen.

As an exercise in concealment, it was bafflingly successful. The crustacean was never seen again – but its memory lived on, especially in warm weather.

Then, there was Tom's very personal driving style. To say that he drove with his foot flat to the floor would be inaccurate: the steel beneath the pedals had long since rusted away, so that he actually drove with his foot through the floor.

This, and a steering rack with more slack than Matahari's knicker elastic, lent the van the handling characteristics of a crippled B52 crash-landing in a field.

Smelly and alarming as the journey was, they nearly died only once. While crossing Dartmoor (the result of a cartographical interpretation error by Martin) they swerved to avoid a sheep and teetered for a moment with two wheels over the edge of a near-vertical embankment.

Martin, ashen-faced, was shaking uncontrollably – but Tom seemed unconcerned.

"I 'ad this dream once that sheep was really aliens from another galaxy. They thought they was goin' to conquer the planet, but when they got 'ere, they found out we was cleverer than them. We just rounded 'em up and made jumpers out of 'em."

"Y'know, that could almost be true," remarked Matthew. "Sheep are weird. It's the eyes. There's a fine line between dreams an' reality."

This was Martin's big chance. "That's right! In fact, wasn't it Confucius who said, 'Once I dreamed I was a man and ever since I've… er… wondered if I'm a man, or rather a butterfly, dreaming that I'm a butterfly… or, um, a man. Something like that, anyway."

And silence descended again upon the van.

The rain started at Liskeard. It was like a lead curtain dividing warm, sunny Devon from grim, sodden Cornwall.

Buffeted by the fists of an 80mph wind, the van lurched wildly across the double white line and back.

The solitary, rubberless wiper, with a sound like sandpaper on teeth, engraved a perfect arc upon the windscreen.

Tom rolled a cigarette with one hand and gazed unseeingly like a hypnotised rabbit at a point one hundred miles in front of his nose.

"It's a wonder you can see where you're going," remarked Martin encouragingly.

"I can't," intoned Tom. "If there's anything travellin' east – anything at all – we're dead."

Martin laughed. "Hah! Well, I trust you, Tom."

"I don't," offered Matthew. "I've been in three really serious accidents with him, an' I know what I'm talkin' about."

The van finally coughed and limped up the Lizard to Porthoustock at 9.30pm.

Martin was tired, depressed, stiff, wet, frightened, depressed, hungry and depressed. He'd have traded in all his brand new gear on the spot to be at home watching *Casualty* with a takeaway pizza and a glass of his mum's homemade dandelion and burdock.

THE RAIN didn't fall. It swept horizontally across the peninsula with a noise like fingernails on corduroy. It didn't make you wet – it blindly ignored your clothes, especially the waterproof ones, and osmosed directly through your skin into your flesh. After five minutes, you turned white and wrinkly, as though you'd fallen asleep in the bath. After ten, your subcutaneous fat layers became saturated and began to swell and undulate grotesquely. After half an hour, your bones were wet. After just one hour, unless medical assistance was forthcoming, you drowned from the inside.

The Branch sat in Long John Silver's Pirate Nosh Spot and surveyed the scene with an equanimity born of years of British diving.

Eventually, Matthew broke the silence: "Remember that time we made five hundred quid fixing propellers in Poole harbour?"

Grunts and nods all round.

"I don't," piped up Martin. "It was before my time. Tell me about it."

"Yeah? Well, it started out quite bona fide, like. We was called over by some ponce in a cravat on a yacht like a Turkish cat house. "I say you fellows," he shouts. "You wouldn't happen to be divers, would you, by any chance?"

"No," we said, "we're the Iraqi synchronised swimming team. Is this the way to Grand Bahama?"

"Anyway, it turned out he couldn't move. He had full power an' everything, but he just wasn't gettin' anywhere. He thought there must be somethin' wrapped round his prop. So I bunged on me tank, popped over the side of the Zodiac and went down to take a butchers.

"What with me being a highly qualified marine engineer and that, it was immediately obvious to me what the trouble was. He didn't have a propeller.

"I saw it soon enough, sitting on the bottom of the harbour – next to the broken split pin.

"I was choked, I can tell you. This bloke looked as if he had more money than sense. I'd been confidently expectin' a sizeable bung for sorting him out.

"I was just ponderin' the gross unfairness of life when I saw the other propeller – attached to the other yacht, moored about 20ft away. Attached, I couldn't help observin', by a very serviceable-lookin' split pin.

"Well, in no time, I'd whacked our bloke's prop on, and as predicted he was generous to a fault.

"We were just castin' off when this twit in a blazer and an admiral's cap hailed us from the next yacht along. 'Ahoy there! I wonder if you frogmen could lend me a hand. I'd make it worth your while!'

"Before the day was out, we'd fixed every yacht in the harbour. Except the last one. Regrettably that one had lost its propeller – almost certainly, we explained to its owner, because of a broken split pin.

"We never got round to divin'. We were heroes. They even threw a party for us at the yacht club. Free booze all night and a roasted pig. Eddie there got off with the Commodore's wife, didn't you, Ed?"

"Yeah. I think she was bored. She yearned for the exotic, for romance, for excitement. I'll never forget those three days we spent together in Winchelsea. She was all woman."

Martin was shocked but, he had to admit, a little thrilled. This was swashbuckling, twentieth century-style. This was piracy, almost, on the high seas. Well, all right, petty fraud in Poole harbour – but it was still more fun than he'd ever had in his six years as Treasurer of Redhill Badminton Club.

These divers were such rum characters – gaily sailing the line between high spirits and criminality with a marvellous, devil-may-care bravado. Wait 'til he told Margaret about them. But then again – perhaps he wouldn't tell Margaret. Not just yet. He wasn't at all sure she'd approve. In fact, he was pretty certain she wouldn't take to them at all. Buckling swashes wasn't her sort of thing. When you really came down to it, Margaret was, well, a bit…

Martin was suddenly suffused with guilt. He'd been about to say "boring". But how could he? She was sweet and sensible and reliable and, after all, she was his fiancée.

Indeed, in six short months, she would be his wife. To his horror, he found that the very word made his palms sweat. *Wife*.

Perhaps learning to dive was a sort of message from God. *Don't throw your life away, Saggers* (why did God always address him by his surname?) *Seek out some adventurous, flashing-eyed diver beauty, a mermaid, a soul-mate who will roam the world and plumb the deep at your side. You never know – she could be closer than you think!*

Martin glanced surreptitiously about him. He could spot no obvious contenders for the role of mermaid/soul-mate. There was

Big Linda, of course. On his first night, he recalled, she'd invited him to buy her a Malibu and absinthe. By closing time, he'd bought her five. She boasted that she'd worked out so hard in the gym she couldn't find a pair of jeans that would fit over her thighs. He suggested that she bought a pair of flares and wore them upside down. Since then, she hadn't so much as acknowledged his existence. Not that he really minded – he'd always found it difficult to envisage sex with a woman whose shoulders were hairier than his chest.

Then there was the Club Thai. She was from Bangkok and so beautiful it was almost painful. When she joined up, two branch instructors fought a duel to decide who would teach her.

But she spoke no English and, worse, her name was Oi.

In this country, sadly, you can't have a serious relationship with someone called Oi.

THE LANGUAGE thing wasn't the main problem. After all, Margaret spoke perfect English. Constantly. In fact, her voice was a sort of aural hacksaw that gradually rasped away at your major nerve bundles until one day they just snapped. So, in many ways, the prospect of zero verbal communication was quite alluring.

It was simply that he couldn't envisage calling to her in a crowded supermarket, or on the jetty at Bovisand: "Oi!" What would people think? And supposing he was cross with her for some reason? He'd have to shout, "Oi! Oi!" It didn't bear thinking about.

He was awakened from his reverie by a crisp, authoritative voice. "Hello. You're new. You're Martin."

The originator of these observations extended a hand. Quite clearly, the shaking of it was not optional. He complied and encountered a grip like an 8lb lobster's.

"Alison," she crisped.

Martin stared at her. She was tall with square shoulders, square hair, boy's hips and "who cares?" glasses. She had strong eyebrows, one of them tilted ironically at him, and a golden down upon her strong brown arms. She smelt faintly of boats.

She was fantastic. Martin loved her instantly and for ever.

"You're diving with me," she added, by way of explanation.

"I don't think... that is to say..." he fumbled. "The marshal says we won't be diving. The weather..."

"Rubbish. The wind's dropped. It's a Seven at the most. Anyway, the marshal is Edwin, and Edwin wouldn't dive a millpond in a heatwave. I've told him I'll take complete responsibility. So get kitted up. I'll see you at the boat in ten minutes."

Martin wrestled with contradictory urges to salute her and kiss her. In the end, he just swallowed and nodded.

"Good," she said, and slid away with that loose-limbed economy of movement one associates with cowboys and Olympic pole vaulters.

"What do you mean, you're divin'?" demanded Matthew. "There's no divin'. It's blowin' a bloody hurricane out there. We just talked to the coastguard. The forecast is so bad, he's going home for the weekend. He says, what's the point of tryin' to guard the coast when you can't even see it?"

"I'm diving with Alison."

"You're WHAT?"

"She seems to think it's fine. She says the wind's dropped."

"Listen, chum, you have no idea what you're letting yourself in for. She's bionic. Impervious to the elements. She once dived on the *James Eagan Layne*, solo, at night in February, and raised it with two Sainsbury's bags and an SMB. Did you know she used to play Octo-slush for Greenland?"

"What's Octoslush?"

"It was like Octopush, but you played it under ice. It didn't catch on. Only five players, the first season. Alison was one of them."

"That doesn't make her…"

"Martin, she used to play naked."

"Right. Well. So she's tough. But I think that might be good for me. And after all, this is my first dive trip. I've been looking forward to this all winter."

"I know. And we want you to be around next winter, so you can look forward to the next summer."

"Come on, Matthew, she can't be that bad." He blushed. "In fact, I rather like her."

"Careful, matey. Her last boyfriend… well…"

"What about him?"

"He disappeared. Nobody knows for sure what happened to

him, but…"

"Tell me. I need to know."

"The rumour around the Branch is… well, we think she ate him. As part of a mating ritual. Like the Praying Mantis. We searched the B&B, but all we found was his logbook. It had teeth marks on it."

Martin sat down heavily. "You're joking."

"We don't joke about cannibalism here, Martin," replied Matthew gravely. "Look, forget diving for today. Come to the pub with us. Noon at The Angry Local. We'll start there and…"

He was interrupted by a crisp, laconic voice: "Not kitted up yet, Martin? Better hurry – you wouldn't want to miss the boat, would you?"

And Martin was lost – washed overboard by a tidal wave of pure, erotic energy into an all-engulfing ocean of desire.

"No, you bet I wouldn't! I want to be well and truly on that, er, boat. So to speak. One hundred per cent! I'll go and take my clothes off. And put on my, er… Goodbye. See you at the bed. Boat." And he stumbled away, blinded by the scarlet mist of love.

"Bitch," said Matthew to Alison.

"Pansy," said Alison to Matthew.

"Mantis," said Matthew.

"Earwig," replied Alison.

Down at the slipway, the sea and the sky had become mixed up. Usually, as you know, they tend to mind their own business. They quietly agree where the surface is going to be, and they stay on their different sides of it. Not today, however. The sea was charging about in the sky as if it owned the place, and the sky was retaliating vigorously by burrowing into the sea and generally tossing it about. It was all rather bad-tempered, and was accompanied by much crashing and slapping and moaning.

Alison, though, seemed completely unaware of this elemental disagreement. She whistled cheerfully as, with one hand, she tossed the fuel tank, Martin's bottle and both weightbelts into the RIB.

"All aboard, me hearty!" she chirruped, dragging Martin over the stern by his whistle lanyard. "Hang on tight – we're going diving!" And with a roar that momentarily drowned out the gale, the boat leapt from the side of the slip and battled its way towards the breakwater and the open, angry sea.

THERE IS an old Chinese proverb (or is it Japanese?): "Make sure you know what you wish for is what you want…" No, that's not it. What it really says (and it's Korean actually) is: "Choose your dreams carefully or you may wake up asleep." Damn, that's wrong, too. And anyway, it's Vietnamese, now I come to think of it.

Still, you get the general idea: Martin Saggers badly wanted to dive. Now, tossed around the branch inflatable by a Force 6 gale and the robust driving style of Alison, Amazonian beauty and alleged cannibal, he was beginning to wonder why.

A huge roller pushed the boat to the vertical and the prop raced wildly in space. "Darning!" bawled Martin into the teeth of the gale.

"No man calls me darling!" bawled back Alison, her hand on her knife pommel.

"No, DARNING! I'm trying to think of other hobbies beginning with D that I could try instead. Drinking sounds especially attractive at the moment."

"Come on, kit up. We're there."

Martin peered into the frenetic maelstrom of air and white water that lashed about him. He pondered how anyone could possibly tell where "there" was. For all he knew, this "there" might be in the middle of Lake Titicaca, or 20 nautical miles east-north-west of Baffin Island.

And yet, magically, "there" was marked by a little buoy, which Alison deftly lassooed with the painter.

Then all was dark and still and cold and Martin was slipping through space in a cloud of tiny diatomic animals interlaced with strings of slime.

The beam of Alison's torch described a foggy arc – then her face loomed close to his, white and beautiful as the moon. He glanced at his depth gauge: 25 metres and falling. Alison clamped his hand to the buoy line.

Staring downwards, Martin could make out canyons and boulders and huge trees of coral – all entirely illusory. And then, suddenly, a huge black shape materialised out of nowhere. Martin nearly jumped out of his wetsuit.

The shape was the forward funnel of HMS *Flatulent*, an A-class frigate that mysteriously sank with no loss of life in 1943.

Martin had never dived on a wreck before, but even he could tell that the years had been remarkably kind to the *Flatulent*. Why, not only was her wire rigging still intact but it was hung with gay little pennants that fluttered in the current.

As he descended slowly past the bridge, he could make out a gleaming brass telegraph and a wheel of polished rosewood.

But the biggest surprise of all awaited him on deck.

"Ahoy there, me hearty!" called the cheery tar who was busy scrubbing the deck with stone and sand.

Even given his limited experience of British diving – two dips in Stoney Cove and a 15-minute eternity under Swanage Pier – Martin recognised that this lay a considerable distance beyond the realms of the normal.

He scrabbled feverishly at his depth and contents gauges: both read zero.

His ears recoiled at a high-pitched, discordant shriek that reminded him first of *One Man And His Dog*, then of a score of black-and-white movies in which Jack Hawkins and Richard Attenborough maintained stiff upper lips while Sam Kydd, with an oily face and a white roll-neck, spouted a chirpy Cockney platitude for every near-miss by a torpedo from the notorious *U-77* and its maverick Junker commander, Reichskapitan Wolfgang von Doppelganger.

It was a bosun's whistle.

Martin glanced around for Alison but she was nowhere to be seen. In slow motion, he vaulted over the rail on to the deck, where a handful of officers saluted him smartly.

An Able Seaman – Sam Kydd, interestingly – helped him off with his aqualung. Jack Hawkins took his arm and, smiling, led him below deck.

"I say, old man, frightfully glad to have you aboard. Fancy a pink gin?"

"N… no thanks. Yes. Please. A big one. Where's Alison?"

"Hmm? Oh, the gal. Positively no gals allowed on board, old chap – you know the drill. Awfully bad luck. Plenty of time for that sort of thing later."

"Later?"

"Certainly, old man. When we reach Valhalla."

"Yes. Valhalla. Of course. That's in…?"

"Norway. That's right. Sort of Norse version of heaven. Bit hard to take at first. Lots of big, fair-haired women with, um, brass knockers, if you get my meaning. And inexhaustible horns of mead. And singing. But it's surprising how you get used to it. Lots of our chaps wound up there. Arctic convoys and so forth."

"Forgive me, Mr Hawkins…"

"Please! Jack!"

"…but what am I doing here?"

"Why, you're enjoying a well-earned snifter in the wardroom of the pluckiest little ship in the King's Navy. Bottoms up!"

"Look here, I'm just an ordinary diver. This is… was… my first proper dive. Where's my kit? Where's Alison? What's happening to me?" Martin's agitation was rapidly escalating towards pure panic.

"Ah. Right. I can see you haven't quite grasped the full implications of your present, er, predicament. Fact is, old boy, you're one of us now."

"You don't mean… I'm…?"

"Quite."

"Did I drown?"

"Good lord, no. None of us drowned. We were only actors, after all. No, I believe your club van hit an oncoming juggernaut near St Austell."

"Then where are the others? Where's Matthew?"

"Completely unscathed, I gather. They write off vans all the time, apparently. Beats me why the insurance companies would touch 'em. Mind, I expect the premium will go sky-high now there's been a… fatality, if you'll pardon the expression. More gin, dear fellow?"

"No. Yes. And Alison?"

"Sort of courier. One of us. Played 'Second Brutal Warder' in *The Cold Titz Story* (certificate 18, video release only)."

Martin sighed and smiled sadly into his drink. "Ah, well. I suppose there's a bright side to all this. At least I won't have to go to the Branch-bloody-AGM and dinner-dance."